THE INTEGRATION
OF PSYCHOTHERAPIES

WITHDRAWN

THE INTEGRATION
OF PSYCHOTHERAPIES
A Guide for Practicing Therapists

Alvin R. Mahrer, Ph.D.

University of Ottawa
Ottawa, Canada

 **HUMAN SCIENCES PRESS, INC.**

Library of Congress Cataloging in Publication Data

Mahrer, Alvin R.
  The integration of psychotherapies.

  Includes bibliographies and index.
  1. Eclectic psychotherapy. I. Title.
[DNLM: 1. Psychotherapy—methods. WM 420 M214i]
RC489.E24M34 1988   616.89'14   87-26091
ISBN 0-89885-412-1

BOOKS BY ALVIN R. MAHRER, Ph.D.

Therapeutic Experiencing: The Process of Change (1986)
Psychotherapeutic Change: An Alternative Approach to Meaning and Measurement (1985)
Experiential Psychotherapy: Basic Practices (1983)
Experiencing: A Humanistic Theory of Psychology and Psychiatry (1978)
(Editor with L. Pearson) Creative Developments in Psychotherapy (1971)
(Editor) New Approaches to Personality Classification (1970)
(Editor) The Goals of Psychotherapy (1967)

CONTENTS

FOREWORD

As I begin to write this foreword for Al Mahrer's new and incisive book, *The Integration of Psychotherapies*, I wonder: Does anyone read forewords? I seriously doubt it, but I will write it anyway. Al has paternally "told" me to write it (cleverly cloaked in an invitation) and reminded me to "enjoy writing it." So whether anyone reads it or not, here's a foreword for my friend and father figure, Al Mahrer.

Being one of those rare humans who habitually reads them, I have acquired a strong distaste for rambling and intellectualized forewords that neglect the person of the author and force us to generalize from a glib autobiography and a 20-year-old photograph on the dust jacket. Instead, I thought that I would enjoy writing a rambling and mildly irreverent foreword that focuses on the person of the author.

A proper introduction of this sort calls for a few words on the man and his work. To begin with, my (real) parents repeatedly instructed me to pronounce the person's name accurately so as not to embarrass myself or him/her. His name is Alvin R. Mahrer. Not really. He prefers *Al* over *Alvin*, since he declares the latter is formal and distancing. I think it's because *Alvin* conjures up images of cute singing chipmunks. It's Al (not Alvin) *R*. Mahrer. He won't tell me what the R stands for: I suspect its one of those embarrassing family names. The trickiest is his last name. Many people, including me, initially pronounce *Mahrer* with a soft "a," like "mare" (a female horse). But the correct enunciation is a strong "a," like "mar" (to disfigure) or "Mars" (a planet and a candy bar). Hence, his offspring, genetic and intellectual, are affectionately known as Martians (Mahrer-tians).

And what of the man behind the name? What kind of person devotes a year of his life to write a book on this topic? Here are a few intriguing personal tidbits about Al Mahrer.

> His beautiful wife is also a psychologist. (Their relationship reminds me of the old saying, "Behind every good man stands a better woman.")
>
> She owns an authentic, honest-to-God jeep (not one of those souped-up yuppie machines).
>
> They own a friendly but incessantly gnawing dog (as evidenced by the bite marks on their house's wood moldings).
>
> He worked for 5 years at the University of Waterloo doing, in his words, "nothing but playing with infants" (earning him the dubious title of "infant psychotherapist").
>
> He professes a "need" to write every day or else suffer from withdrawal symptoms.
>
> He types most of his correspondence on an ancient electric typewriter and bothers the secretaries for antique typewriter ribbons.
>
> He teaches at the first fully accredited bilingual clinical psychology program in Canada (but he barely speaks French).

Last year I presented a colloquium at the Centre for Psychological Services at the University of Ottawa. We sauntered from the Centre over to the tasteful and reserved faculty dining club. The coat-check woman asked Professor Mahrer, "May I take your coat?" Al replied, "Will you give it back?" During lunch (I had the fish, Al had the soup) he ruminated aloud about this woman's meager salary and encouraged us to tip her generously. On leaving, Al asked the woman directly, "Would you mind telling me how much you get paid for doing this?" The woman was taken aback not by the directness of the question as much as by Al's childlike innocence and concern. This direct, wide-eyed inquiry into the heart of the matter has characterized his prolific research and writings. What are the goals of psychotherapy? How does one actually *do* experiential psychotherapy? What are "good" moments in psychotherapy? And so on.

Now Al Mahrer brings his refreshing and concerned directness to psychotherapy integration, a movement experiencing unprecedented growth and in need of direction. Consider, for example, that in the past 10 years alone several nonideological psychotherapy associations were organized, the National Institute of Mental Health (NIMH) sponsored a workshop on research in psychotherapy integration, an international journal on the topic was founded, and, by my count, over 50 books on the synthesis of various theories and formats were published. Moreover, between one-third and one-half of contemporary psychotherapists align themselves with "eclecticism" or, increasingly, with "integrativeness."

As editor-in-chief of the *Journal of Integrative and Eclectic Psychotherapy*, I have met hundreds of people praising the merits of informed pluralism in psychotherapy and have read countless manuscripts advancing superordinate integrative frameworks. These proponents, however, have almost uniformly been oblivious to the underlying critical issue of *how* to integrate. They have consistently placed the proverbial cart before the proverbial horse.

Not Al Mahrer. He strikes at the heart of the matter with three organizing questions. What are the meanings and strategies for integrating psychotherapies? Which meanings and strategies are usable and which are less so? What are the consequences for the field of psychotherapy of pursuing these strategies? He reviews six strategies for integrating psychotherapy, and then recommends we embrace two and one-half of the six.

Technical eclectics and theoretical integrationists alike will find direction here. One of his proposals is to develop a large pool of concretely specific operating procedures—a strategy traditionally associated with eclecticism. The second proposal entails the construction of substantively new theories of psychotherapy—a strategy now linked to integration.

Not that you must accept his conclusions to profit from the book. On the contrary; I enjoyed *The Integration of Psychotherapies* thoroughly, but disagreed vehemently with Al on several occcasions. For example, his conceptualization of the sixth strategy—Diagnose-the-Problem and Prescribe-the-Treatment—is off the mark. This meaning of integration, for me, is Understand-the-Person and Orient-Therapy-to-the Person. We obviously cannot fully appreciate a person solely through DSM-III (or DSM-IIIR), but need to understand a client's phenomenal world and interpersonal drama. *This* clinical understanding, not discrete diagnoses, can be translated into more prescriptive therapeutic stances and interventions.

Whether you agree or not with Papa Al (or me), I trust you will savor his insightful account and benefit from his well reasoned recommendations. Al Mahrer is one of the most intriguing people I have ever encountered. Not surprisingly, he has provided one of the most enlightening books on psychotherapy integration I have ever read.

John C. Norcross, Ph.D.

INTRODUCTION

Integration among psychotherapies is exceedingly widespread, whether it is called rapprochement, eclecticism, or bridge-building, whether it is fueled by factors that are political, professional, economic, or conceptual, whether it is welcomed or resisted, whether or not it is supported by research, and whether its consequences for the field of psychotherapy are seen as dire or salubrious (Arkowitz & Messer, 1984; Beutler, 1983; Diamond, Havens, & Jones, 1978; Frank, 1982; Frankel, 1984; Garfield, 1980; Goldfried, 1980, 1982b; Goldfried & Newman, 1986; Goldstein & Stein, 1976; Held, 1984; Lazarus, 1976; Luborsky, 1985; Marmor & Woods, 1980; Norcross, 1986a; Prochaska, 1979; Prochaska & DiClemente, 1982; Ryle, 1982; Wachtel, 1977).

More than merely acknowledging that integration is widespread, more than discussing how and why it *is* so widespread, surveys indicate that perhaps somewhere between a quarter and a half of psychotherapists avow what may be roughly termed an eclectic or integrative orientation, and the proportion is probably on the increase (Garfield & Kurz, 1976, 1977; Jayaratne,

1982; Nash, Norcross, & Prochaska, 1984; Norcross, 1986c; Norcross & Prochaska, 1982; Prochaska & Norcross, 1982, 1983; Shemberg & Leventhal, 1978; Smith, 1982; Smith & Kraft, 1983).

Throughout this book I will use the term "integration" to refer to what psychotherapists do when they put together something from this approach and something from that approach. It may be done in a way that is creative, organized, conceptual, pragmatic, rigorous, scientific, formal, constructive, or it may be done in a way that is at the other extreme. Some carefully distinguish between such terms as integration, eclecticism, rapprochement, and similar terms. For example, Norcross (1986c) provides a careful exposition of the meaning, history, and overview of eclecticism in psychotherapy, and Goldfried and Newman (1986) do the same for integration. Nevertheless, I am going to risk the loss of some precision by using the single term, "integration." My aim is to review this whole trend toward integration, to present six different meanings and strategies of integration, to point out the consequences of each meaning and strategy on the field of psychotherapy, and to make a series of recommendations so that psychotherapists can carry out constructive integration while sidestepping and declining what I regard as fruitless or destructive integration.

These recommendations are given in the final chapter. If you are tempted to glance at the action proposals I am going to urge you to carry out, take a look at the final chapter. Is is short and terse. It is comprised only of the overall conclusions and recommendations. On the other hand, if you prefer to work your way through the discussion and presentation of arguments, then postpone the last chapter till last. In either case, the purpose of this book is to present you with a series of action-oriented recommendations for your serious consideration. I hope that many of you will see your way to carrying out these recommendations. I regard the whole matter of the integration of psychotherapies as very serious indeed, both for better and for worse, and I hope that we psychotherapists can take an active stance in assuring that it is for better.

SIX DIFFERENT STRATEGIC MEANINGS OF INTEGRATION

What are the meanings of "integration"? Each of the following chapters will concentrate on a different strategic meaning. Here is preview: (a) Integration means developing new theories of psychotherapy that organize or integrate a family of psychotherapies. This leads to a reduction in the number of therapies in the field. (b) Integration means that most therapies pick and choose from a public marketplace of quite concrete and specific operations and procedures and things that therapists do. The various therapies retain their essential differences; but there is greater exchange or integration at the operational level of what therapists actually do. (c) Integration means that something is done about the large number of languages or vocabularies there are in the field of psychotherapy. Maybe we can work toward a more or less common vocabulary, or at least identify words and terms that seem to have much the same meaning. (d) Integration means developing a single super-psychotherapy, one comprehensive framework that integrates all or most others. (e) Integration starts with the belief that there are lots of commonalities across the various therapies, common dimensions that are shared by the various therapies. According to this meaning, therapies are combined or integrated along these commonalities and we should end up with a smaller number of more integrated therapies. (f) Integration means that all or most of the therapies are available as treatments once we diagnose the problem. Then we can select the most appropriate treatment or therapy for the given problem. Here are six different strategic meanings of integration, each with its own version of what would and should happen to the field of pschotherapy.

When you think of the integration of psychotherapies, you probably picture a few major, comprehensive psychotherapies replacing a disorganized fragmentation of lots of different approaches. If I am successful, when you finish the book you will picture a small number of theories of human beings (for example, an existential-humanistic theory of human beings, a psychoanalytic theory of human beings, a learning theory of human beings). For each large theory of human beings, you will picture a broad and comprehensive theory of psychotherapy, a substantively new theory of psychotherapy that integrates a family of psychotherapies sharing the same larger theory of human beings. This is one way I hope you will think of integration. You will also picture a large, open, public marketplace of concretely specific things that psychotherapists do (I will refer to these as "operating procedures"), and you will be picturing each theory of psychotherapy gradually adding or discarding a few of these operating procedures as they prove useful or useless for that theory. This is the second way I hope you think of integration when you finish the book.

If I am successful, the phrase "integration of psychotherapies" will not be connected with the hope of a single common psychotherapeutic vocabulary or language. It will not mean some single super-psychotherapy, a monolithic common approach that covers most of our psychotherapies. It will not mean constructing new and bigger therapies out of the supposed commonalities across most therapies. Nor will it mean combining all the therapies into a large package of available treatments to be used on a selective basis once the problem is identified or diagnosed. I hope you will be ready to discard these strategic meanings of integration.

INTEGRATION IS EXCEEDINGLY WIDESPREAD

My impression is that most psychotherapists are engaged in their own form of integrating therapies. In an informal, casual way, most practitioners quietly and gradually carry out one or more of the various meanings of integration over the course of their careers. What is distinctive is that the integrative movement is taking on a formal public quality, but when we combine formal and informal integration, it certainly appears that most psychotherapists are indeed engaged in a good measure of integration.

Formal integration

Formal integration refers to therapists who identify themselves as using as using an approach that includes something from a number of therapies. It is quite respectable today for a therapist to indicate that she does therapy by combining a little psychodynamic with some client-centered and Gestalt. Or he uses some hypnotherapy, neurolinguistic programming, and desensitization. Because there are so many therapies, it is attractive and easy to name the three or four different components of one's overall approach. It is fashionable and reasonably descriptive. It is a brand of formal integration because so many therapists publicly acknowledge that they integrate several therapies in their practice. Indeed, it is becoming so common that therapists who claim to carry out a single therapy are easily slotted as elitist or limited. To assert that one is a rational-emotive therapist, or a psychoanalytic therapist, or an Adlerian, is to place oneself above the pack, well behind the pack, or distinctly *away* from the pack. When a therapist says, "I am a Gestalt therapist," or "I am a psychoanalyst," the sense is almost that of being specially trained, a purist, belonging to a particular school, and probably being somewhat preeminent.

On the other hand, therapists who combine Gestalt therapy or psychoanalytic therapy with others are today gaining for themselves that same sense of being specially trained ("I have mastered psychoanalytic and hypnotherapeutic methods"), of being a purist who belongs to a special school ("I am competent in all the genuinely deep and intensive therapies"), and as being somewhat preeminent ("I have all the tools of my trade, rather than being limited to just those of, for example, Gestalt or psychoanalytic therapy"). Formal integration has gone way beyond merely labeling oneself eclectic.

What is more, formal integration is organized. If you come out of the closet and publicly show yourself as an integrationist, you can join your own academy, belong to your own society, and have your own journal. You can belong to the International Academy of Eclectic Psychotherapists. You can belong to the Society for the Exploration of Psychotherapy Integration. You can subscribe to the *Journal of Integrative and Eclectic Psychotherapy*. Formal integration is exceedingly widespread.

Those who are committed to formal integration also are asking the key questions whose answers have direct implications for the academic and internship training of psychotherapists, for research on psychotherapy, for certification and credentialing as psychotherapists, and for the very practice of psychotherapy itself. These integrationists are concerned about the fragmentation into many splinter therapies, and they are asking how we can work toward a smaller number of better therapies. They are asking how the many therapies can be combined to provide the best possible service to patients. They are asking what the commonalities are across the various therapies. They are studying ways of building helpful and useful bridges across therapies. They are asking which therapies are most appropriate for what kinds of problems. They are studying the ways in which new therapies can be developed by integrating features of therapies belonging to some generic family. All in all, these issues and questions indicate that formal integration is exceedingly widespread and bears strong implications for the field of psychotherapy in general.

Informal integration

Since around 1950 we have witnessed an explosion of audiotapes, videotapes, one-way observation windows, demonstrations, and workshops. What we therapists do is now out of the closet and open to public scrutiny. The leading proponents of most therapies give workshops and demonstrations of what they do. There are commercially available audiotapes and videotapes of hundreds upon hundreds of therapists plying their trade. Training and supervision and consultation among peers and colleagues rely upon audiotapes and videotapes, as well as direct observation of actual psychotherapeutic work. Published verbatim transcripts are increasingly common. Therapists and therapeutic approaches that keep their work hidden must count on cultish excuses for justifying the sacrosanctity of the session. Psychoanalytic therapists are among the most adroit at hiding their work behind solid justifications. Nevertheless, many psychotherapeutic doors are now open for others to see just what is occurring in the actual practice of psychotherapy.

Informal integration means that psychotherapists are carrying out some form of integration without ever talking about it openly. As therapists listen to tapes of what others do, watch videotapes, attend workshops and demonstrations, read verbatim transcripts, they tend to pick up a thing or two. The more we know precisely what goes on in other therapies, the more we do a little informal integrating here and there in our own work. By knowing what all these well-known therapists actually do, it is so easy to do a little Perls, add a bit of Ellis, take a little from Bugental, handle this the way Wolpe does, use a trick from Strupp, and so on and on. Informal integration is a casual consequence of seeing and hearing good therapists work.

We can still assert that we are cognitive behaviorists or Jungian analysts, client-centered or psychoanalytic, multimodal or eclectic. Nevertheless, when you take a close look at what most therapists actually do, there is a great deal of informal integration going on.

It seems to me that if we combine both formal and informal integration, about all that we have excluded are the exemplars of the various approaches and some of their devout followers. Integration is exceedingly widespread. Because it is so widespread, it calls for careful consideration. Because so many psychotherapists are engaged in formal and informal integration, they are in a position to shape the effects that the various meanings and strategies of integration can have on the field of psychotherapy. And we are now ready to state the purposes of the book and the questions we want to answer.

PURPOSES AND QUESTIONS

In an incisive analysis of both elegant and crude integration efforts, Schacht (1984) concludes that answers to the key questions hinge upon a careful examination of the strategies that are used in the integration of therapies. Because there is so little written on these strategies, my aim is to try to answer those key questions by proposing the various strategies that are used to integrate psychotherapies. Accordingly, the purpose is to answer the following questions:

What are the various strategies that are used for integrating psychotherapies? I propose that there are six different strategies, each with its own rationale, its own meaning of integration, and its own methods and procedures for carrying out the strategy. It is easy to talk about integrating psychotherapies as if there were one meaning, one vision of what this is. But that is too glib. If we can identify different strategies, it becomes clear that we have quite different meanings of integration, quite different visions of what integration means. As psychotherapists, we are formally or informally engaged in our own strategies of integration. In order to discuss the matter of integration, it helps to be clear on the various strategies that are used for integrating psychotherapies.

How do the several strategies fare in a comparative analysis of their feasibility, workability, and chances for success in integrating psychotherapies? My conclusion is that three warrant consideration as eminently feasible, workable, and effective, while the other three are much less so.

What are the likely consequences for the field of psychotherapy of pursuing each of the strategies? My conclusion is that each of these strategies will have pronounced effects on the field of psychotherapy, and that these effects will vary with the strategy that is used. Depending on which strategies are used, the likely consequences may be a reduction or a mushrooming proliferation in the sheer number of therapies, progressive development within and between larger families of psychotherapy, or a competitive struggle for superiority across most psychotherapies. These consequences are serious. Differences between strategies make a difference.

Is integration good or bad for the field of psychotherapy? My answer is that if we took at the likely consequences of each of the six meanings and strategies of integration, some consequences are good and some are bad. What is more, the good and bad consequences link up nicely with the particular strategies and meanings of integration so that the answer can be given. If we follow particular strategies and meanings, the consequences are good. If we follow the other strategies and meanings, the consequences are bad. The differences do indeed make a difference.

On the basis of our study of the various strategies for integrating psychotherapies, what recommendations are warranted? The book ends with a series of recommendations directed toward the psychotherapist. They are in the form of action proposals for each psychotherapist—practitioner, teacher, supervisor, and clinical researcher—to consider seriously, to modify and it is hoped to carry out. In an important sense, this book is dedicated to presenting you with these recommendations. I did not start out with these recommendations. They took shape gradually as I tried to draw conclusions at the end of each chapter and as I studied these conclusions in writing the final chapter.

A Personal Stake in the Integration of Psychotherapies

My work consists of studying and developing experiential psychotherapy. I do this by going deeper into experiential psychotherapy itself, and also by studying what goes on in other psychotherapies. Where, then, does the integration of psychotherapies fit in? As an experiential psychotherapist, and as a clinical researcher who likes to look at other therapists, I have a personal stake in this whole matter.

To begin with, I find that "integrationists" convey an attitude that I like. In general, they believe that there are lots of different therapeutic approaches, that there is something probably pretty good in many of them, that we still have a way to go in developing fine psychotherapies, and that each of us believes our way is best. There is an easy mutual acceptance, a collegial understanding of differences, an enthusiasm for talking with one another. It is precious when passionate zealots of different therapies share these beliefs.

Secondly, I am concerned about our field of psychotherapy. Although I love experiential psychotherapy, I worry that the field of psychotherapy is in pretty bad shape generally. We have plenty of students, plenty of practitioners, plenty of patients, and the overall life-style of psychotherapists is good. But I am concerned that there are too few really fine practitioners, effective artisans who are masters of the craft. As you will see, I believe that the consequences of our integrative strategies are mixed. Some of the consequences will be bad for the field of psychotherapy. But some consequences will be good. I believe that integrationists are dealing with many of the crucial questions for our field, and I have faith that much of what they are trying to do will have favorable consequences for the field of psychotherapy. Accordingly, the recommendations I offer at the end of the book are with the hope that they will help to guide the field of psychotherapy in directions that are good for the field.

My personal stake also comes from a commitment to some of the integrative strategies. My own experiential psychotherapy was developed and continues to grow by studying other therapies and therapists. I study the writings of other therapists, both their theoretical writings and their clinical descriptions of just how they do psychotherapy. I am committed to research that examines in detail the actual work of therapists outside the experiential approach. In part, this is to learn more about psychotherapy in general, and in part this is to learn more about how experiential psychotherapy can grow and develop.

Finally, I am involved in the training of both predoctoral and postdoctoral psychotherapists, and it is here that some issues of integration have special relevance (cf. Norcross et al., 1986). It is interesting that those who are part of the integration movement span the various psychotherapy-related professions and disciplines, including psychology, psychiatry, social work, education, and others; yet each of these professions has its own distinctly separate and unintegrated training programs (Mahrer, in press). Should doctoral training be in the generic profession and discipline? I am in favor of this position. Should postdoctoral training concentrate on a particular psychotherapeutic approach, or should postdoctoral training cut across the various approaches? I am in favor of postdoctoral training in specialized approaches such as psychoanalytic or experiential or rational-emotive or Gestalt therapy. Should postdoctoral training include faculty from the various psychotherapy-related professions and disciplines? I am in favor of this position. As someone who is involved in doctoral and postdoctoral training, I have a serious concern with the many training issues directly related to the integration of psychotherapy.

All in all, I have a personal stake in the integration of psychotherapies. Indeed, I believe that most psychotherapists share their own personal concern with these issues, whatever your psychotherapy-related profession, whether you are a psychotherapy practitioner or teacher, supervisor or clinical researcher, whether you are an integrative therapist or follow some other approach. This is why my audience is all psychotherapists.

THE AUDIENCE: ALL PSYCHOTHERAPISTS

My audience is all psychotherapists. The reason is that each of you is engaged in some kind of integration of pyschotherapies. It may be very subtle, but it is occurring in each of you. If you are a psychotherapist, or counselor or psychoanalyst or case worker or behavior modifier, it is almost certain that you are already engaged in some kind and some degree of integration. My aim is to suggest how and why to go about it in ways that are fruitful.

I had started writing this book for that small group of psychotherapists who were involved in the organizational movement dedicated toward integrating psychotherapies. Actually, it began as a paper. But the more I became involved in the paper, and the more I discussed the paper with my partner, colleague, friend, and wife, Dr. Patricia Gervaize, the more the issue grew. As the readings and the note-taking grew over the years, so did the breadth of the audience. As I really got into the writing of the manuscript, I found myself writing for a number of groups of psychotherapists. One group includes those who are learning about psychotherapy. I hope that you read this book in the course of your graduate training, your internship or field training, where you are face to face with many of our psychotherapies. Another group includes the smaller number of you who teach and supervise psychotherapy. I hope this book will help you and your students find a way of structuring the field of psychotherapy so that teaching may be a little easier and a little different from the traditional covering of the various approaches to psychotherapy. The smallest group I had in mind includes those who are likewise concerned with the issues and the strategies of integrating psychotherapies. I have in mind here the members of the Society for the Exploration of Psychotherapy Integration, and also the contributors and readers of the fine *Journal of Integrative and Eclectic Psychotherapy*. Finally I had in mind those clinical researchers who seek to study psychotherapy so as to learn more about useful and effective practice.

Yet the largest audience is each practitioner. The reason is that you are the one who is more or less engaged in some kind of integration. When you look back a number of years, you have most likely changed in your way of doing therapy. When you look across at your colleagues, you most likely do therapy in a way that is somewhat different. These changes and differences are predominantly the product of some kind of integration. At the end of the book I have a series of recommendations. They are addressed to you. If you seriously consider these recommendations, I believe that integration will proceed in ways that are good for us and for the field of psychotherapy. That is why my audience is all psychotherapists.

A Short Walk through the Book

The organization of the chapters is quite simple. The first six chapters each present a different strategy and meaning of integration. Within each chapter, the strategy and meaning of integration is described in sufficient detail to carry it out, if it is workable, and to provide sufficient reasons not to carry it out, if you agree that it is unworkable. Also, each chapter concludes with a section on the consequences of that strategy and meaning on the field of psychotherapy.

Chapter 1 describes how a new theory of psychotherapy is developed in a way that integrates a family of therapies sharing the same theory of human beings. A second strategy and meaning of integration (chapter 2) is for the various therapies to engage in free trade at the level of concretely specific operating procedures. Chapter 3 is concerned with integrating therapies at the level of their vocabularies, and discusses one limited and one more grandiose way of doing this. Except for the more grandiose meaning of an integrative vocabulary, these three strategies and meanings of integration are regarded as promising and workable, with favorable consequences for the field of psychotherapy.

Chapter 4 discusses the strategy and meaning of developing a super-framework that is to integrate all or most other therapies. The fifth strategy and meaning of integration (chapter 5) is to identify commonalities across all or most therapies, and then to integrate therapies along these commonalities. The sixth strategy and meaning (chapter 6) consists of diagnosing the problem and then prescribing the most appropriate and effective of the available therapies. I regard these three strategies and meanings as much less promising and workable, with generally unfavorable consequences for the field of psychotherapy.

The final chapter presents the conclusions in the form of answers to the leading questions presented earlier. Chapter 7 ends with a series of recommendations for psychotherapists. Those recommendations are in the form of actions that each psychotherapist is invited to carry out.

Chapter 1

INTEGRATIVE DEVELOPMENT OF SUBSTANTIVE NEW THEORIES OF PSYCHOTHERAPY

The first meaning of integration involves the development of a substantive new theory of psychotherapy that blends or combines or organizes several therapies into something new. The key word is "theory," for the strategy is to develop a new theory of psychotherapy. The new theory is integrative because it provides the family framework for the therapies that now belong to this new family. I regard this as the most elegant meaning and strategy of integration.

In a way, the next topic might be to describe this strategy in detail, to show what it is and how it works, and to give some examples of new theories of psychotherapy that have been developed by means of this integrative strategy. However, before we get to this topic, there are three questions to be answered. (a) How does a theory of psychotherapy differ from a theory of human beings? If we are dealing with the development of a substantive new theory of psychotherapy, it is necessary to distinguish between theories of psychotherapy and theories of human beings. (b) What are the components of a theory of psychotherapy? In order to develop a new theory of psychotherapy, we should have a clear idea of what its components are.

In order to develop a new theory of psychotherapy from bits and pieces of other theories, we should have a picture of what these bits and pieces are. (c) How may a theory of psychotherapy be judged as new and complete? If the aim is to develop a theory of psychotherapy, there should be some way of judging the product as new and complete. Then we can turn to the first strategy, to what it is and how it works, and some examples.

A THEORY OF PSYCHOTHERAPY AS DISTINGUISHED FROM A THEORY OF HUMAN BEINGS

There are theories of human beings, and there are theories of psychotherapy. A theory of psychotherapy is different from a theory of human beings. Clinical theorists who study the whole matter of integration of psychotherapies tend to draw a sharp distinction between a theory of human beings and a theory of psychotherapeutic practice (Frankel, 1984; Franks, 1984; Franks & Wilson, 1979; Goldfried, 1982b, Jacoby, 1975; Krasner, 1978; Mahrer, 1978a, 1983a; Messer & Winokur, 1984). Whether we refer to it as a theory or conceptual system of human beings or personality, it makes sense to distinguish between it and a theory of psychotherapy.

There are psychoanalytic theories of human beings, social learning theories, humanistic theories, trait theories, existential theories, analytical theories, sociological theories, organismic theories, biosocial theories, field theories, learning theories, and so on. Theories of human beings deal with questions and issues that are distinct from the questions and issues of theories of psychotherapy. For example, theories of human beings deal with questions and issues that involve the nature of feelings, what causes them, what they are understood to be, what good and bad feelings are like and how they differ; the nature and function of the human body, its structure and workings, how it relates to behavior; human relationships and interactions, how they arise and change; the nature of reality, how it is constructed and used; the nature of social phenomena, their structure and origins and how the person fits in; human behavior, its determinants and relationships with internal and external events, its origin, maintenance, and modification; the nature of optimal functioning, what it is and how it may be achieved; human development and change from before conception throughout life, the nature of infancy and the plateaus or stages of development; the structure or model of human being or personality, the components and relationships among components, the nature of basic personality events; the philosophy of science of the nature of events and basic events, of relationships among sciences; paradigms, methods of inquiry, and research study. Theories of human beings have their own questions and issues to deal with.

A theory of psychotherapy is not the same as a theory of human beings. Its components are different, and so too are the issues and questions with which it deals. Every theory of human beings may imply or give birth to a theory of psychotherapy. Every theory of psychotherapy comes from or fits into a larger, encompassing theory of human beings; but a theory of human beings is not the same as a theory of psychotherapy.

What is a theory of psychotherapy? If one of the strategies for integrating psychotherapies is the integrative development of a substantively new theory of psychotherapy, we should be able to name the components of a theory of psychotherapy. Most likely they are different from the components of a theory of human beings.

COMPONENTS OF A THEORY OF PSYCHOTHERAPY

What constitutes a theory of psychotherapy? What are its components? There certainly are lots of theories of psychotherapy. There are innumerable reviews and surveys and critical analyses and discussions of them. There is a great deal of research from and about them. I had expected that there was a rich literature on what their components are. Such a literature exists with regard to theories of human beings. If such a literature exists with regard to theories of psychotherapy, I have yet to come across it.

I therefore called and corresponded with many of the leading figures in this field. They confirmed what I had begun to suspect, namely that there is precious little literature on this topic. There ought to be a good measure of concern with what comprises a theory of psychotherapy. There were plenty of hints, but little or no concentrated examination of this topic. An example of a more or less inadvertent backing into this matter is Orlinsky and Howard's (1987) outlining of the background for their own therapeutic system. They started with what they consider the common features of many therapies, and used their own reading of these common features as both the cornerstones of their own therapeutic approach and as a provisional statement of the components of a theory of psychotherapy. Here is my summary of Orlinsky and Howard's provisional list of components (Mahrer, 1987):

1. A theory of psychotherapy sets forth the therapeutic contract, including the purpose, format, terms, and limits of the therapy.
2. A theory of psychotherapy identifies the therapeutic interventions, including the means and methods of arriving at a diagnostic determination of the problem, and also the help-providing methods and operations of the therapy.
3. A theory of psychotherapy describes the nature of the therapeutic bond or emergent relationship between therapist and patient, including the working alliance, mutual empathic resonance, and sense of mutual affirmation.
4. A theory of psychotherapy includes the nature of personal self-relatedness, including the manner in which therapist and patient experience and manage their own thoughts, feelings, and self-definitions in the therapeutic encounter.
5. A theory of psychotherapy identifies the therapeutic realizations, including the helpful impacts that occur in the sessions, and the changes in the patient outside therapy.
6. A theory of psychotherapy sets forth the interrelationships among these five components, describing how each components works in relation to the others.

Orlinsky and Howard offer one attempt to set forth the components of a theory of psychotherapy. What follows is my own attempt, offered along with a healthy suspicion that I may have overlooked a rather respectable body of writings on the subject. I propose that a full-fledged theory of psychotherapy should include seven components. These are given in Figure 1. The components are to be present in any theory of psychotherapy, from Gestalt theory to eclectic theory, from psychoanalytic to experiential therapy, from client-centered to rational-emotive theory. These are the cornerstones for developing an integrative new theory of psychotherapy.

1. The useful material to be elicited

A theory of psychotherapy identifies the kind of material that is to be elicited from patients. It names the kind of material that it regards as useful, worthwhile, relevant, important, therapeutically meaningful. It names the kind of material the patient is to provide, express, talk about, show, do.

The material may be useful for getting some idea of what the patient is like, for allowing change to occur, or for any other purpose. Therapies may agree that this kind of material is quite useful. Or therapies may differ widely on what kind of material is regarded as useful. It does not matter. What does matter is that each theory of psychotherapy includes some *identification* of the nature and kinds of useful material that is to be elicited by and in that psychotherapy.

What is more, each therapy has implicit or explicit rules for naming the conditions under which certain kinds of material are regarded as useful. Some therapies say that before therapy starts, here is the useful material to be elicited in pre-therapy intake or evaluation sessions. Some therapies hold that in the beginning of sessions, or in early phases of therapy, these other kinds of material are regarded as useful. Once therapy gets started and is rolling along, here is yet another kind of material that is regarded as useful. Some therapies have more detailed conditions, so that there are different kinds of useful material

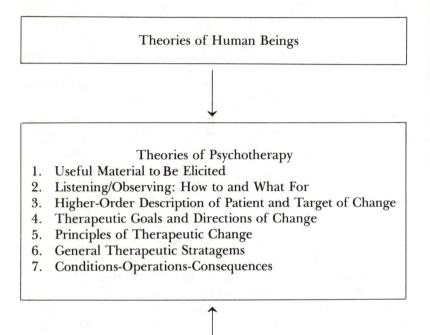

Figure 1. Theories of Psychotherapy: Their Components and Relations with Theories of Human Beings and Operating Procedures.

when the patient is upset, or heading toward the end of therapy, or when particular therapeutic operations are working or not working. Whatever the conditions, each theory identifies the kinds of material that it labels as useful.

Here are some examples of the kinds of material that some theories elicit as useful while other theories would regard as not especially useful: dreams that the patient had a few days or so before starting therapy, a physician's report about the patient's general medical condition, the flow of free associations, the specifics of the patient's birth events, success or failure in carrying out the assigned homework, descriptions of the immediately ongoing bodily sensations, recollections of parental injunctions, familial pressures for the patient to fulfill a given social role, how the patient responds to a blank and neutral therapist, talking about other persons rather than oneself, talking about oneself rather than other persons, expressions indicating degree of reality contact, scores on vocational tests, childhood thoughts about sexual fantasies related to the opposite-sexed parent, favorite figures from the field of literature, description of the patient's and partner's reactions to a graded series of sexual tasks that were carried out following the last session, thoughts and ideas flowing out of a state of hypnogogia, coping self-statements, expressions of dysfunctional and irrational cognitive ideas and beliefs, emotional reliving of childhood traumas, learning how to fatigue and then relax muscles, feelings and reactions to the therapist's office.

Each theory has its own explicit or implicit list of the kinds of material the patient should be providing, and each theory has its own ways of eliciting the kinds of materials it values. While some kinds of elicited material may be valued by several different theories, this overlap is quite small compared to the distinctive nature of each therapy's elicited material. From the very beginning, and throughout the course of therapy, each theory tends to elicit its own brand of useful material the patient is to provide and express.

In the experiential theory of psychotherapy, the useful material is the immediate experiencing. It is the undergoing of the experiencing of hurtfulness, light-hearted joy, bubbling sexuality, nagging doubt and uncertainty, aloneness, loyalty and devotion, disorganized chaos, control and power. The useful material is the having, the undergoing, the expressing of some kind of experiencing. Because experiencing rarely occurs all by itself, it needs some kind of props and scenery or situational context in which to enable the experiencing to occur (Mahrer, 1978b, 1978c, 1980, 1983a, 1983b, 1986a, 1986b). In other words, some sort of material is also useful to provide for the truly useful experiencing in this person right now. Accordingly, the patient may be a little child trying to hold onto the dog's tail, or listening to his wife explaining how badly he treats her, or seeing the image of the tree he just planted, or sensing the antagonism from the guy on the street who wanted some money, or driving his new sports car, or recollecting the way his father got so maudlin whenever he drank a lot. But the genuinely useful material is the experiencing that accompanies whatever the patient's attention is profitably directed toward.

A theory of psychotherapy tells the kinds of material that it regards as useful, important, significant. It tells what kinds of material the patient is to provide. The useful material may vary with the patient, with what is happening right now, with the stage or phrase of therapy; but each theory identifies the useful material that is to be elicited.

2. Listening/observing: How to and what for

Each theory of psychotherapy tells the therapist how to listen and observe, and what to listen to and observe. When the patient talks and behaves, how do you listen? How do you observe? What do you listen to, and what do you observe? Even if you invite the patient to talk about some problem or to tell something about her father, do you listen as if you are the one she is addressing? Do you listen from the vantage point of a removed party who is here to examine what she says about her father? Do you listen by saying the words right along with her? Do you listen with all your attention on her, or is most of your attention on something else, such as you own flow of private thoughts? A theory of psychotherapy tells where the therapist is to place herself in order to listen to what the patient is saying.

How do you observe things as she is talking and behaving? If the theory says that observations of the patient are important, then you should probably keep your eyes open. An experiential therapist has her eyes closed, so she probably would miss a lot of things you would observe with your eyes open. Do you sit behind the patient who lies on a couch, or do you sit face to face? Each position lets you observe some things and miss others. A theory of psychotherapy tells how to observe.

Each theory should also tell you what you are to listen to and observe. Her is where theories differ a great deal. Whatever your theory says you are to listen to and observe become the important data. For example, if you are on the lookout for indications of nystagmus or stuttering, you may be working with data from neurology or speech pathology. On the other hand, you may listen and observe in such a way that your data include splits in awareness, irrational beliefs, pathological indicators, archetypal material, deeper experiencings, symbolic indicators of the patient-therapist relationship, and on and on. Each theory tells how to listen and observe, and what to listen for and observe.

The experiential theory of psychotherapy tells the therapist to listen to and observe what the patient says and does by allowing what the patient is saying and doing to be as if it is coming in and through the therapist (Mahrer, 1978c, 1983a, 1986a). It is as if the therapist is saying and doing it along with the patient. It is as if it is all coming in and through the therapist in the very same way, with the same tone of voice, the same volume and amplitude, same pauses, same words, same everything. It is as if the therapist were joined into or aligned with the patient so that what comes from the patient is as if it is coming in and from both of them. By this "experiential listening" the therapist has the experiencing which accompany what is coming in and through both patient and therapist. The therapist experiences sorrow or pride, toughness or jealousy, hurt or giddiness. This way of listening uses experiencings as the data. This way of listening is a powerful means of sensitizing the therapist to the ongoing flow of experiencings. The experiential theory of psychotherapy shows the therapist how to listen to what the patient is saying and doing, and what to listen for.

Each theory of psychotherapy is to tell the therapist how to listen to and observe the elicited material that theory holds as relevant. Some theories emphasize observational data, and they therefore tell the therapist what observable material is to be elicited by the therapist, how to observe what the patient says and does, and how to make sense of what is observed. The theory may invite the therapist to observe splittings between what the patient is doing and nonverbal bodily actions such as foot tapping, looking to the upper right when seeking answers, or clenching of the fist. Other theories emphasize observations of body postures relative to those of the therapist. Depending upon the kind of material which is to be observed, the therapist may sit face-to-face with the patient, have physical contact with the patient, complement the patient with other family members, emphasize mutual dyadic eye contact, and so on. Theories that highlight such observational material will tend to decline modes of listening that minimize the eliciting of such observations, for example, by sitting adjacent to the patient with both patient and therapist having their eyes closed, as in experiential psychotherapy, or by having the patient on a couch with the therapist sitting behind the patient, as in psychoanalytic psychotherapy.

However, most theories include a heavy emphasis on *listening*. Accordingly, the theory tells how to listen and what to listen for. In order to obtain the material that most theories listen to, the therapist and patient are to be in a very particular postural relationship to one another, they are to engage in a conversation with one another, and they are to have most of their attention on one another. No matter what the patient talks about, the preponderance of both the patient's and the therapist's attention is to be on one another as the patient talks.

Then the theory says that the therapist is to listen in some particular way that is designed to hear some particular thing. For example, the therapist is to listen for dysfluencies in speech patternings, or for underlying irrational beliefs, or for signs of schizophrenia, the presence of neurological blocks, the implicit feeling in the patient's words, the hidden voice of the "child" or "parent," the permeability of the patient's personal constructs, or for allusions to the patient's deeper feelings toward the therapist. The theory tells the therapist what to listen for, and how to listen in order to obtain this material. Each therapy has a *way* of listening that fits the kind of material that therapist is to listen for. Even the physical aspects of the office fit into the therapy's way of listening. In psychoanalytic therapy, if the therapist is to listen for the flow of the patient's free associations, it makes sense for the patient to lie down and for the therapist to sit behind the patient, allowing the therapist's attention on the flow of associations to be undisturbed by a back-and-forth interaction with the patient. Similarly, in experiential psychotherapy, if the therapist is to share in the patient's experiencings, it makes sense for therapist and patient to have their eyes closed, and for the two of them to attend to whatever the patient's attention is focused upon. It is the job of the theory to identify how to listen and what to listen for. It then becomes the job of the therapist to figure out the most useful way of doing this—face-to-face or not, eyes open or closed, sitting or reclining, and so on. If a theory tells the therapist to listen for the patient's childhood fantasies about the opposite-sexed parent, or for the subtle neurological blocks, or for the implicit feeling in the patient's words, perhaps the most fitting way of listening would be otherwise than face to face with the patient, each attending to and talking to one another.

In general, however, a theory of psychotherapy tells the therapist how to listen and observe, and what to listen for and observe. When a patient is saying and doing something, even for just 5 to 20 seconds or so, each theory will listen and observe in its own distinctive way. Where one theory says the patient is experiencing defiance, another will say that the patient is recounting historical information about her father, a third will hear the patient showing signs of secondary stuttering, another will identify indications of therapeutic resistance, still another will focus on the patient's topdog/underdog polarity. Yet the patient has said and done one 5-to-20-second statement which is received and listened to and observed in singularly different modes. Each theory has a component that tells how to listen and observe, and what to listen for and observe. It is surprising how different this second component is from theory to theory.

3.   Higher-order description of patient and target of change

A theory of psychotherapy offers a framework for describing the patient and the target of change. It has some system, some categories, a framework of concepts, constructs, terms, words to describe the patient and the target or object of change. Once you elicit some useful material from and about the patient, and once you listen to and observe that material in some way, how do you put it together so as to say something about the patient and the target of change? A theory of psychotherapy shows the therapist how to do this. The third component, then, consists of some frame of reference, some vocabulary, for describing the patient and the target of change.

As soon as you start describing the patient and a selected-out target of change, you are operating out of some theory. You are functioning within some particular higher-order descriptive framework. It is a higher-order framework when you go beyond simple descriptions, relatively free of any particular theory, and use the descriptive system provided by that framework. You may describe the patient as having a slight limp or being a little over 6 feet tall, and these descriptions are not especially particular to the system of any given theory of psychotherapy. But all higher-order descriptions come right out of one theory or another.

Within a psychodynamic-psychoanalytic theory we may describe the patient as a borderline personality or a regressed schizophrenic or a narcissistic personality. These are useful descriptions within one theoretical framework and, while every theory is to provide some way of describing patients, each theory is quite free to provide its own descriptive system. For example, the various theories may describe the same patient with such different descriptive phrases as being an incest survivor, caught in the throes of a negative transference, pursuing fictional goals, having a limited behavioral repertoire, showing low self-esteem, high arousal level, manifesting poor effectance motivation, showing phobic behavior, lacking assertive behaviors, disputing irrational beliefs, showing dichotomous reasoning, using reinforcing self-statements, manifesting a weak ego, showing reaction-formation, moving from the child to the parent ego state, stroking, crossing transactions, conforming to the cultural stereotype, fixated at the anal level, focusing on a felt meaning, manifesting motor disturbance, being hypomanic, being in a state of anergia, having rigidity in the muscular armor. There are several descriptive frameworks represented here.

A theory has terms such as these to enable the therapist to grasp the patient, to understand and describe the patient. Some system or framework for describing the patient is provided by a theory of psychotherapy. It may be exceedingly complicated or rather simple, but it is a part of every theory.

Within its own perspective, each descriptive system for describing the patient and the target of change may well be quite accurate. In terms of the higher-order description, the patient certainly is a borderline personality or an incest survivor or has a deeper potential for critical complaining. There really *is* an irrational belief about having to be loved to be of any worth, or there really *is* a weak ego, or the person really *was* the victim of a schizophrenogenic mother. In terms of targets of change, the person really needs a more accepting attitude toward the terminal illness or the person really should be able to be in crowds without being so scared or the patient really has a persistent headache or low back pain or a bad attitude toward minority groups. Each theory provides a way of describing the patient and the target of change which may well be accurate, within its own perspective.

What is more, each theory will almost certainly have its own way of describing patients. Its way of describing a patient may be convincingly apt and accurate, and quite different from that of another theory. As the patient says and does things, and as the therapist listens to and observes this material, the theory tells how to organize the data, how to put it all together to describe the patient in its own distinctive way. A theory that describes the patient as being "fixated at the anal level" would probably not be prepared to describe the patient as "using reinforcing self-statements." Each theory has its own particular way of describing patients, and there usually is only a measure of overlap.

Description of the target of change is generally a part of the overall descriptive system of the theory. In other words, each theory describes what is to change. There are no problems or difficulties or targets of change independently sitting there, free of the descriptive system of some theory. Problems, difficulties, and targets of change are the achievements of some particular theory's descriptive system. Each theory is prepared to describe certain targets of change, and these are limited to the given theory. The actual words used in describing targets of change tell us which theory is at work. Accordingly, only *certain* theories would be prepared to describe the target of change as the borderline condition, the fear of high places, the opening of one's spiritual side, the fear of the male role, the need to be free of the feminine role, the speech defect, the oedipal problem, poor work habits, truancy, lack of assertiveness, or whatever the theory is prepared to describe as targets of therapeutic change. It may be called the problem, or difficulty, or target of change, but each theory of psychotherapy provides concepts and constructs to *identify* it, give it *existence*, and describe *what it is*.

The experiential theory of psychotherapy does not describe patients or targets of change in terms such as schizophrenia, weak egos, assertive behaviors, motor disturbances, poor work habits, or truancy. Instead, the core description of patients and targets of change involves experiencings (Mahrer, 1978a, 1983a, 1984; Mahrer & Boulet, 1986). The theory describes patients in terms of their potentials or possibilities for experiencing. For example, a patient may be described in terms of a potential for experiencing loving concern, caring, or a potential for experiencing control and domination. Some potentials are direct determinants of behavior. They are at the operating surface and comprise the functioning, behaving, operating personality. Some potentials are deeper, outside of the "operating domain." The potential for experiencing loving concern and caring may be at the operating level or at the deeper level. What is important, in describing patients, is mainly the nature and content of the experiencings. From these potentials for experiencing, we can construct a picture of this person, including the nature of the relationships among the potentials, the behaviors which flow from the operating potentials, and the nature of the worlds which are constructed by the potentials.

In the experiential theory, the targets of change likewise

refer to these potentials for experiencing and the nature of their relationships. Every potential for experiencing can occur in its good form, can relate to other potentials in an integrative manner, can be at the operating level rather than a deeper level, can be outfitted with its own appropriate behaviors, and can construct and exist in its own appropriate external world of situational contexts. Neither our descriptive system in general nor our way of describing targets of change involve psychodiagnostic terms and categories, dysfunctional or problematic behaviors, symptoms, behavioral disorders, or any of the essential parts of the descriptive systems of other theories of psychotherapy.

Every theory of psychotherapy offers a way of describing patients and describing the targets of change. Some are simple and some are complex. Some are distinctive and some overlap somewhat with others. Some are presented as only one of many ways of providing higher-order description of patients and the targets of change, and some are presented as the solid single truth. Yet each theory of psychotherapy includes a component consisting of a way of making higher-order description of the patient and of the target of change.

4.   Therapeutic goals and directions of change

The first three components enable the therapist to elicit useful information, to listen and observe, and to describe the patient and target of change. The fourth component activates the therapeutic process, sets it in motion, and guides where it goes. It is the basis for virtually everything the therapist does to carry out the process of change. Each theory of psychotherapy must include a statement of its therapeutic goals and directions of change (Figure 1). By "therapeutic" I mean that the goals and directions of change are connected to the therapy rather than merely a loose recounting of whatever the parent theory of human beings holds as a general setting forth of whatever the parent theory of human beings regards as its version of mature, healthy, optimal behavior or way of being or adjustment or the good life.

Suppose we consider three levels of abstraction or generality of goals and directions of change. At one extreme are the particular goals and directions of change for this patient right now. At the other extreme are the general goals and directions of change, the picture of the good life of mature, healthy, optimal functioning that is provided by the parental theory of human beings. There is an in-between zone. It consists of the goals and directions of change set forth by the given theory of psychotherapy. It is consistent with the goals and directions of change for a particular patient and for people in general. Yet it fills the gap between these two extremes.

Each parental theory of human beings has something to say about the good life, the mature and healthy existence, optimal functioning. For example, in the existential-humanistic theory of human beings, optimal functioning consists of a state of actualization and integration; it is the goal of life, the plateau of highest attainment as a human being. Other theories of human beings see normal, mature, healthy, adjustive, optimal being in their own distinctive ways. They may describe this state in terms of social commitment, reduced tension and anxiety, full selfhood, pleasure-principle functioning, maximization of instinctual gratification, congruence of expectations and occurrences, ego integrity, acquisition of adjustive behaviors, congruence between self and ideal self, and lots of other formulations about what human beings can become in terms of maturity, health, normality, adaptation, adjustment, or optimal functioning. These are not therapeutic goals and directions of change. They are bigger and broader ideas which serve as an encompassing framework. Each theory of psychotherapy has its own set of therapeutic goals and directions of change that fit into and are congruent with the bigger and broader picture of maturity, health, normality, adaptation, adjustment, the good life, or optimal functioning provided by its parent theory of human beings.

An experiential theory of psychotherapy holds that there are four classes of therapeutic goals and directions of change (Mahrer, 1967, 1983a, 1985, 1986a). These are framed so that it is possible to evaluate the degree to which they have been attained in work with a given patient: (1) There will be actualization of the good form of the operating domain, including (1.1) heightened experiencing of the good, integrated form of the operating potentials, (1.2) an increase in good-feelinged, bodily sensations of actualization, and (1.3) the occurrence of new behaviors for the good form of the operating domain. (2) There will be integrative relationships with deeper potentials, including (2.1) the replacement of disintegrative feelings with integrative feelings, (2.2) the extinguishing of externalized and internalized forms of the deeper potential, (2.3) the extinguishing of disintegrative relationships with the external world, and the occurrence of integrative relationships, (2.4) a decrease in disintegrative behaviors, and (2.5) an increase in integrative behaviors. (3) Deeper potentials will become operating potentials, including (3.1) the occurrence of new operating potentials, and (3.2) the occurrence of new ways of being and behaving for the new operating potentials. (4) The old operating domain will extinguish, including (4.1) the extinguishing of the operating domain's external world, and (4.2) the extinguishing of the operating domain's behaviors.

Once the experiential therapist has some picture of this patient, of this patient's potentials for experiencing, the theory provides principles for generating a picture of what this particular person is capable of becoming. We can see the optimal state which is possible for this person. This picture constitutes the therapeutic goals and directions of change. As the therapist gains increasing information about this patient's potentials for experiencing, there are symmetrical changes in the generated picture of what this person can become. These are the therapeutic goals and directions of change provided by the experiential theory of psychotherapy.

Similarly, each theory of psychotherapy provides a statement of its therapeutic goals and directions of change. Depending upon the particular theory of psychotherapy, this may include such features as the reduction of symptomatology, the reduction of defenses, reduced anxiety, heightened sexual fulfillment, the replacement of irrational ideas with rational ideas, increased self-acceptance, enhanced repertoire of coping behaviors, greater adjustive external relationships, increased competence of social functioning, greater ability to confront the demands of life, increased social commitment, reduced psychopathology, and so on.

The statement of therapeutic goals and directions of change

are in between the general classes provided by the larger theory of human beings and the specific goals and directions of change as applied to this particular patient right now. Yet these are the goals and directions of change that enable the therapist or patient or someone else to evaluate whether change has occurred, and if so, whether it is change in the direction of the valued goals and directions of change. This is the basis for evaluating outcome, progress, movement, process, improvement, change.

Perhaps more importantly, it is the presence of therapeutic goals and directions of change that allows the whole therapeutic process to be set into motion. There is little room for change without some notion of therapeutic goals and directions of change. Every theory of psychotherapy provides the therapist with a way of applying this framework to that patient so that there are therapeutic goals and directions of change, and so that the processes of therapeutic change are set into motion.

5.   Principles of therapeutic change

A theory of psychotherapy sets forth its principles for bringing about therapeutic change. A theory may state its principles rather generally or quite concretely. A theory may rest its case on one grand principle of therapeutic change, or it may have several. If a theory has several principles of change, they are generally placed in some sort of order or sequence. Yet every theory of psychotherapy offers one or more principles of therapeutic change. Without these, the therapeutic process is static. By means of these principles, therapeutic change can move ahead.

If we organize the various therapies into major families, we can ask each family what it counts upon as its main principle of therapeutic change. Looking at the principles of change in this way, Gelso and Carter (1985) propose three main principles: insight, experiencing or awareness, and learning:

> The internal client mechanism that is most important in psychoanalysis is *insight* . . . In contrast, the humanistic

therapist sees client *experiencing or awareness* as the key to constructive and durable change . . . For the learning therapist, the critical dimension of change is *learning* (including conditioning). (p. 233)

But we can take a closer look at each of these major principles of therapeutic change, and identify a larger number of more specific principles. For example, one may speak generally of learning and of the modifying of the cues upon which behavior is held as contingent. If we take a closer look, it is possible to identify principles of behavioral shaping, of change through reinforcement and punishment, through modeling, desensitization, classical conditioning, discriminative learning, avoidance learning, and so on. The general principle of insight and understanding may be seen as including particular kinds of insight and understanding such as insight into genetic psychoanalytic factors, insight into one's personal constructs or irrational beliefs or general life philosophy or relationship with the therapist or family role relationships. Once we take a closer look at grand principles such as learning or insight, we can identify a rather large number of more specific principles of therapeutic change.

Other schemas yield still different principles for effecting therapeutic change. For example, therapeutic change may be said to come about through principles of persuasion and suggestion, corrective emotional experiences, the adoption of more effective personal and life philosophies, self-exploration, and so on. Some therapies count upon the therapeutic relationship as an effective avenue of therapeutic change, and even then there are several component principles for how change occurs through this relationship. For example, it may be said to occur through the development and resolution of the transference neurosis, or through the establishment of a genuine, empathic, unconditionally accepting atmosphere, or through the encountering of each participant's deeper personality processes.

Theories that accept several principles or subprinciples of change generally include some way of ordering or sequencing. For example, the experiential theory accepts a single grand principle of change: therapeutic experiencing. But that is comprised of four subprinciples, four kinds of therapeutic experiencing, and these are organized into a general sequence (Mahrer, 1978b), 1983a, 1985, 1986a; Mahrer & Gervaize, 1986). As given in Figure 2 (p. 79), each session follows the same sequence. The session opens with whatever the patient is experiencing right now, and the aim is for the patient to allow this experiencing to reach a level of genuine strength, fullness, amplitude, or saturation. This is the first kind of therapeutic experiencing, and it consists of the attaining of a strong level of experiencing. Once this occurs, patient and therapist work together to change the quality of this experiencing. It is to be carried forward into its good or "actualized" form. It is to be placed into a friendlier and more "integrated" relationship with whatever potential is deeper. This second principle is referred to as the "appreciating" of potentials for experiencing. One of its important bonuses is that whatever potential for experiencing may be "deeper" is lifted up, made substantially more available.

This opens the way for the third kind of therapeutic experiencing in which the person is given an opportunity to disengage from the ordinary, continuing personality, and to enter into the wholesale being of the deeper potential for experiencing. Here is a radical shift from one personality into another, into one that was "deeper." The fourth and final kind of therapeutic experiencing provides the person with a taste and sample of what it can be like to be this deeper potential within the context of the extratherapy world. It is as if the person gets an experiential feel of what it can be like to leave the therapy room and to enter the extratherapy world as this radically new personality who can be and behave in its own way. These are the four subprinciples that comprise the larger principle of change through therapeutic experiencing.

Whether or not a theory of psychotherapy orders the principles of therapeutic change in some pattern or sequence, each theory includes its own principle or principles of how therapeutic change occurs. Whether or not a theory is explicit in their identification, every theory of psychotherapy includes one or more principles of how therapeutic change can and does come about.

6. General therapeutic stratagems

Each of the components so far gets the therapist ready for doing something. The theory identifies the target of change, e.g. the stuttering or the readiness to rebel at the spouse's commands or the anxiety at being in an enclosed situation. The theory sets the therapeutic goals and directions of desirable change. The theory even tells what principles are available in order for change to come about. But what does the therapist do? Each theory or psychotherapy includes therapeutic stratagems for what the therapists is to do. These consist of programs of things to do, but only in a general way. As indicated in Figure 1, we must distinguish between general therapeutic stratagems and the concretely specific operating procedures that comprise these general therapeutic stratagems.

In the parlance of psychotherapy, words such as "techniques," "methods," and "procedures" are commonly used, but fail to distinguish large and loose general therapeutic stratagems from these concretely specific operations. For example, in discussing the problems in integrating psychodynamic and behavioral approaches, Levis (1970) speaks of "techniques" and "procedures" which rather clearly refer to general therapeutic stratagems rather than concretely specific operations: ". . . it is important to be cognizant of the fact that the arsenal of the behavior therapists comprises a number of different techniques. Systematic desensitization, implosive therapy, and operant conditioning procedures are only three such examples" (p. 534). Of course there is no law prohibiting using the word "technique" when referring to systematic desensitization, implosive therapy, and operant conditioning. Whatever words are used, I prefer to distinguish between implosive therapy, which I would class as a general therapeutic stratagem, and the concretely specific operating procedures that make up the nuts and bolts of implosive therapy. I would also refer to systematic desensitization and operant conditioning as "general therapeutic stratagems" rather than as "techniques" or "concretely specific operating procedures." Similarly, in arguing for what he terms "pragmatic blending," Halgin (1985) includes the following "techniques" as borrowed from psychodynamic, interpersonal, person-centered, and behavioral approaches: direction, exploration, modeling, cognitive restructuring, and educative interventions. A distinction can be drawn between these and their working nuts and bolts—the concretely specific operations by which the therapist does "cognitive restructuring" or "direction." We need a distinction between the larger programs (general therapeutic stratagems) and the working procedures.

Once we stay at this somewhat general level, and once we accept the idea of therapeutic stratagems, then we can see that there are lots of them: educative intervention, dream analysis, cognitive restructuring, assertiveness training, contingency management, thought stopping, cognitive problem-solving, self-exploration, carrying forward of experiencing, transference analysis, relaxation training, flooding, emotional problem resolution, stress management, focusing, guided fantasy, neurolinguistic programming, psychodrama, co-counseling, social awareness training, bibliotherapy, hypno-suggestion, counterconditioning, operant conditioning, biofeedback, participant modeling, and on and on.

There are many ways of naming these general therapeutic stratagems, of classifying them, and of distinguishing them from on another and also from their component nuts-and-bolts working operating procedures. In any case, a theory of psychotherapy includes one or more general therapeutic stratagems as the means whereby therapy actually takes place. Theories will differ on what these stratagems are, but every theory tells the therapist that these are the stratagems for doing the therapy.

7.   Conditions-operations-consequences

The final component of a theory of psychotherapy is a kind of manual for carrying out the therapy. The theory is to say that under this and that condition, here is what you are to do, and then this or that is the likely consequence of doing it. In other words, the theory provides a working manual of conditions-operations-consequences (Mahrer, 1983; Orlinsky & Howard, 1987). If a theory does not include this component, the therapist would not know what to do, or when to do what, or what to try and do it for. Some kind of manual of instructions is a necessary component of any theory of psychotherapy. The "conditions" may be big and broad or they may be quite detailed and specific. At the big and broad end, the condition may be when therapy is just getting started, when you are heading toward termination, or when the patient is given this or that psychodiagnosis. At the more detailed and specific end, the condition may refer to when the patient is on the verge of crying, when the patient is silent after the therapist has just delivered a fine interpretation, or when the patient is living in a scene of being a little child in bed with her cousin and giggling her head off as they are playing wickedly exciting sexual games with one another. Whether big and broad or detailed and specific, the conditions refer to what is going on now, and they invite the therapist to do something appropriate under this or that condition.

The "operations" refer to what the therapist is to do under those conditions. Again, what the therapist is to do may be framed more generally or more specifically. It may be as general as some therapeutic stratagem or it may be as specific as a given operating procedure, but the therapist is given some kind of direction that under these conditions here is what you do. Sometimes the direction spells out specifically that under these conditions you are to disclose something of yourself, or you are to give further instructions, or you are to interpret or reflect or tell the patient to say it again with more feeling. Sometimes what the therapist is to do is indicated more generally. Rather than detailing what concretely specific operation the therapist is to carry out, the theory merely tells the therapist that under these conditions the therapist is to undertake a general therapeutic stratagem such as assertiveness training or self-exploration, and the therapist should know the concretely specific operations that must be used in carrying it out.

The "consequences" define what should occur when the therapist carries out these operations under the given conditions. If I do this, under these conditions, the patient should then be like this, or do that, or change in this way, or undergo that. The patient should self-explore or have stronger experiencing or provide this information or have insight into that issue or start crying or focus on that feeling. These are specific in-session consequences that can be seen after the therapist does this operation. However, the consequences may be broader, along the lines of traditional outcome consequences which are to occur in the patient's extratherapy world in between sessions or when therapy is finished. Accordingly, the consequence should be the trying out of the new behavior, extinguishing of the self-defeating behavior, reduction of the headache, heightened communication in the family. Consequences may refer to what happens in the session, or later, outside the sessions.

The conditions-operations-consequences are like an instructional manual for carrying out the therapy. If they are spelled out, the therapist can do the therapy. If they are not spelled out, the therapy is mainly a static bunch of parts and pieces. Any theory of psychotherapy should include this component.

These, then, are the proposed seven components of any theory of psychotherapy. I suggest that it is these components that make a body of ideas into a theory of psychotherapy, and that distinguish it from a theory of human beings or any other kind of theory.

These are what I propose as the seven components of a theory of psychotherapy. They should be present in a psychoanalytic theory of psychotherapy, a behavioral theory, a Gestalt theory, and every other theory of psychotherapy. Indeed, every candidate for a theory of psychotherapy should have something to say about each of the seven components. Now we are ready to deal with the topic of this chapter, i.e., the integrative development of substantive new theories of psychotherapy.

How to Judge the Candidate as a genuine Theory of Psychotherapy

Every so often, a candidate claims that it integrates a number of other theories into a substantively new theory of psychotherapy. Now that we have a provisional set of components that should be in any theory of psychotherapy, we can judge whether the candidate qualifies as a genuine theory of psychotherapy. Looked at in a different way, if a theorist claims to have integrated a number of theories into a substantively new theory of psychotherapy, the claim should show that the proposed new theory has the following characteristics.

It should have reasonably high goodness-of-fit with the parent theory of human beings

In order for the supposed new theory of psychotherapy to qualify, it should have a reasonably good fit with a parent theory of human beings. As long as a theory of psychotherapy seeks to bring together pieces of different therapies, the implied parental theories of human beings should fit together congruently.

Consider that one holds to a psychoanalytic theory of human beings, and the new integrative theory of psychotherapy incorporates a therapeutic stratagem of covert desensitization. Does the conceptual framework of covert desensitization have high goodness-of-fit with the psychoanalytic theory of human beings? If the answer is yes, then one has succeeded in meeting this criterion. If the answer is no, there are at least two options. One is to reject the therapeutic stratagem of covert desensitization; it does not fit, and there is no new integrative theory. The other is to modify the psychoanalytic theory of human beings so that the modified theory of human beings squares well with the conceptual framework of covert desensitization. If there is no appropriate modification in the psychoanalytic theory of human beings, and if that theory of human beings is unable to accommodate covert desensitization, then there is no room for a new integrative theory of psychotherapy.

Integrating several theories of psychotherapy can be accomplished when each theory of psychotherapy has high goodness-of-fit with a single parent theory of human beings. Indeed, it seems to me that integration will occur gradually and naturally when several theories of psychotherapy connect to the same parent theory of human beings. It may take a while, but if three or five or more somewhat different behavioral theories of psychotherapy all share a single learning theory of human beings, integration will take place, and the direction will be toward a single integrative behavioral theory of psychotherapy.

On the other hand, theories of psychotherapy that connect with significantly different theories of human beings cannot be integrated unless there is some change in the parent theory of human beings. It will not work. But this does not mean that integration is restricted to families of psychotherapy that share the same parent theory of human beings. It does mean that the part that is to give is the theory of human beings. Here is where exciting and creative change can and does occur. There is nothing fixed about a theory of human beings. Even slight modifications in theories of human beings have rich implications for changes in their theories of psychotherapy and also in providing plenty of room for integration of theories of psychotherapy. The answer lies in modifying, improving, developing our parent theories of human beings.

If we modify the psychoanalytic theory of human beings, the way is clear to see what theories of psychotherapy may thereby be integrated into a substantively new theory of psychoanalytic therapy. For example, if the more or less traditional psychoanalytic theory of human beings can be modified on the basis of new object-relations thinking, then the exciting implications include the integrative development of a substantively new theory of psychotherapy which connects well with the modified psychoanalytic theory of human beings.

My own way of doing therapy was a gradually evolving loose package of components, all within an even looser reading of existential-humanistic notions about human beings. I found myself drawn toward particular methods of listening to what patients said, toward attractive directions of therapeutic change, toward explicit principles of therapeutic change, and especially toward what seemed to be effective therapeutic stratagems—yet none of these seemed to connect well to existential-humanistic notions about human beings, and even seemed to conflict at too many points. The choice was to continue muddling around in arriving at some way of doing therapy, to try and ignore the jarring disconnections with what I understood as an existential-humanistic theory of human beings, or to revise the existential-humanistic theory of human beings. My choice was to modify the theory of human beings. I ended up with a revised existential-humanistic theory of human beings (Mahrer, 1978a) that provided a reasonably high goodness-of-fit with an experiential theory of psychotherapy (Mahrer, 1983a, 1986a).

It does not matter where we start—with the theory of human beings and working down to ways of doing therapy, with a theory of psychotherapy that seems to integrate with several others, or with a number of theories of psychotherapy that seem to call out for integration. Regardless where we start, there must be a reasonably high goodness-of-fit between the theory of psychotherapy and the theory of human beings. Yet we have few ways of gauging the degree to which there is such a good connection. To what extent does the psychoanalytic theory of psychotherapy really fit in with the psychoanalytic theory of human beings? Jacoby (1975), for example, argues that throughout Freud's writings there is serious divergence between the two:

> From his early writings to his last no attempt is made to reconcile individual therapy with the "metatheory" of psychoanalysis; they exist in contradiction. . . . Changes in the former can proceed without changes in the latter because the locus in each case is different: one takes the individual as ill, the other civilization as ill. Measures taken to cure the individual are not identical with those taken to "cure" the civilization; to a point they diverge. (pp. 120–121)

It is hard enough to study the goodness-of-fit between implosive therapy and its parent learning theory of human beings, or between classical psychoanalytic therapy and the psychoanalytic theory of human beings, or between any theory of psychotherapy and its parent theory of human beings. But if we seek to develop a new integrative theory of psychotherapy out of several other theories of psychotherapy, it is important to demonstrate that the new theory of psychotherapy has a high goodness-of-fit with some parent theory of human beings. If it doesn't, then it either is not a solid integrative theory, or some change must be made in what is taken as the parent theory of human beings. If it does, then what has almost inevitably happened is that the new integrative theory of psychotherapy has been developed out of theories of psychotherapy bearing high goodness-of-fit with the same parental theory of human beings;

or that there has explicitly or implicitly occurred a significant modification of a parent theory of human beings. In any case, the demonstrated goodness-of-fit with a parent theory of human beings is one way of judging the candidate as a genuine theory of psychotherapy.

It should provide a clear statement of its components of a theory of psychotherapy

It is rather easy to say that we have integrated psychodynamic and behavioral therapies into something new, that we have integrated several experiential therapies into something new, or that we have integrated biofeedback, Gestalt, client-centered, and encounter therapies into a new blend. But if the claim is that the product is an integrative theory of psychotherapy, then there should be a spelling out of the components of the new theory of psychotherapy so we can say that this really is a theory of psychotherapy and we can say this new theory is *different* from its integrated therapies. This exercise demonstrates the extent and the nature of how and where the supposed new theory of psychotherapy is indeed new. If you believe that you have integrated psychodynamic and behavioral therapies into something new, then this will be the proof.

This exercise shows whether the combination has yielded a genuinely new theory of psychotherapy or whether one has merely adopted a soft stylistic feature that is more or less characteristic of some *other* theory. Some therapies have been characterized as having the therapist be relatively active, or benignly gentle, or rather brusque and abrasive. If a psychoanalytic therapist is occasionally brusque, that hardly qualifies as integrating psychoanalytic therapy and Fritz Perls's Gestalt therapy or Albert Ellis's rational-emotive therapy. A psychodynamic therapist may occasionally be warmly gentle without integrating psychodynamic and client-centered therapy into something new.

Many therapies start with what has been achieved in the session and consider the implications for changes in the patient's extratherapy daily life, ". . . to help the patient systematically to apply the lessons learned in the sessions to his or her daily life" (Wachtel, 1984, p. 46). This is a stylistic feature of at least hypnotherapy, Gestalt therapy, rational-emotive therapy, experiential therapy, and behavior therapy. Adding this stylistic feature may not qualify as developing a whole new integrative theory. If the stylistic feature translates into a significantly new component of a theory of psychotherapy, then it qualifies as perhaps a new theory of psychotherapy blended from a number of theories. But if the added feature is merely a stylistic innovation without comprising a new component, then there has not been an integrated development of a substantive new theory of psychotherapy.

It should identify the "ripple effect" of an integrated component on the other components

In a way, developing a substantive new integrated theory of psychotherapy is easier than one may think, for merely adding a new component to some established theory of psychotherapy has a ripple effect throughout the other six components. If a new component is integrated into a given theory of psychotherapy, the new theory of psychotherapy can be shown to be quite new by identifying all the ways in which the new component makes for changes in all the other components.

Suppose that you are a more or less traditional behavior therapist who describes patients mainly in terms of the behavioral problem and the behavioral constructs related to that problem. You are not especially familiar with the current version of the *Diagnostic and Statistical Manual of Mental Disorders,* and you are really not skilled at the diagnostic differentiation between the various kinds of "serious disturbances" such as "paranoid schizophrenia." But that does not matter, because your behavioral theory of psychotherapy proceeds right along without using the *Diagnostic and Statistical Manual of Mental Disorders.*

Now suppose that you introduce one little new wrinkle to your higher-order description of patients. You accept the psychodiagnostic nomenclature and describe a patient as a paranoid schizophrenic. After all, lots of behavior therapists use psychodiagnostic labels. So you follow suit and allow a paranoid schizophrenic label into one small component of your behavioral theory, namely your higher-order description of the patient (Figure 1). Is this an innocent little addition? Not at all, for the ripple effect will exert pressures to modify dramatically our entire theory of psychotherapy. As Messer and Winokur (1984) point out, each of the several theories of psychotherapy has ". . . a particular model of understanding and organizing data . . . that affects what they accept as data, where they look for it, and ultimately, how they treat their clients" (p. 64).

Now that you have admitted paranoid schizophrenia into your theoretical house, that will exert a profound effect on the useful material you elicit from your patients (see Figure 1). More than your ordinarily useful behavioral data, you really should elicit a whole new slab of material related to the psychodiagnosis of your patient's mental disorders. That makes a big difference in the useful material you elicit. You also must listen to and observe your patients in a way that is sensitive to symptoms of psychopathology and psychodiagnostic indicators. By admitting paranoid schizophrenia into your theory, you certainly will have to modify your therapeutic goals and directions of change to include the reduction of psychopathology; your paranoid schizophrenic should become less paranoid schizophrenic. Also, you will of course add the therapeutic stratagems that are effective in working with paranoid schizophrenics, and, in each of the elements of the conditions-operations-consequences, the diagnostic state of your patients will play a most important part. All you did was add one little shard to one component, and now you have a wholesale ripple effect which alters your whole behavioral theory of psychotherapy. There almost always is a big ripple effect of adding just a little to one component.

This is why so many therapists are insistent on preserving the components of their own theory of psychotherapy. There is a real basis for zealously guarding a given theory, for the apparently innocent addition of a component from an alien theory *may* well generate a substantively new theory of psychotherapy. For example, Gill (1984) holds that transference is precious to a psychoanalytic theory of psychotherapy, and therefore Wachtel's (1977) efforts to introduce elements from behavior therapy are seen by Gill as tantamount to a wrenching change in the psychoanalytic theory of psychotherapy. The changes not only eclipse the precious transference, but effectively open the way to the rippling blossoming of a substantively new theory of psychotherapy which is *no longer psychoanalysis.* I agree with Gill that innocent inserts can have pronounced consequences on the theory of psychotherapy.

Once a therapist adds something new, something borrowed from another theory of psychotherapy, judging the quality of the substantive new theory means identifying the ripple effect on all other components. Typically, the apparently innocent addition of a single new piece means the generation of a quite new theory, and this ripple effect is to be *identified,* and *spelled out.*

It should specify the conditions-operations-consequences interrelationships

Above all else, if a theory of psychotherapy is indeed substantively new, it should show how it makes a difference in what therapists do, the conditions under which they do it, and the consequences of doing it. This is the acid test. Otherwise, the purported new integrative theory is generally *just a new way of talking about* or conceptualizing any or all of the components of a theory of psychotherapy.

I suspect that most "new" integrative theories of psychotherapy are not new in prescribing what therapists do, when they do it, and the consequences of doing it. What is new is the *claim* that the theory is new, often coupled with a few new *terms* here and there. What is new is how the therapists *talk about* what therapy is all about, while the actual conditions-operations-consequences remain virtually intact.

One of the sore problems in the field of psychotherapy is that so few therapies actually spell out the conditions-operations-consequences (Mahrer, 1983a, 1985; Mahrer, Brown, Gervaize, & Fellers, 1983; Mahrer, Nadler, Dessaulles, & Gervaize, 1987; Mahrer, Nadler, Gervaize, & Markow, 1986). Most theories are extremely loose in specifying what the therapist does, under what conditions the therapist is to do this, that, or something else, and the immediate and/or long-term consequences of doing it. If the new theory allows these to be *spelled out,* that alone stamps it as having the quality of a substantively new theory of psychotherapy. Even better would be to compare the new with the old conditions-operations-consequences in order to mark it as new.

These are four ways of judging a supposedly new integrative theory as a genuine theory of psychotherapy. Every time that someone claims to have integrated several therapies into a single approach, it would be helpful if the claim were accompanied with a statement of how the new theory squares with some parent theory of human beings, a statement of each of the components of the theory of psychotherapy, a statement of what is integrated from other therapies and how those integrated items exert ripple effects on all the other components, and a statement of its own new conditions-operations-consequences. Then the candidate can be pronounced as a genuine theory of psychotherapy, new and different from those it integrates. I am proposing that we apply these four criteria to each new candidate.

So far, I have managed not to talk about how to go about this strategy of the integrative development of substantive new theories of psychotherapy. I have said that if one should somehow be brought forth, there are ways to recognize it and do a good job of judging it as a substantively new theory. I have also said that it should certainly be distinguished from a theory of human beings, and that it, like any theory of psychotherapy, should have particular components. Now we can turn to the question of how one can go about the job of developing a theory of psychotherapy that truly integrates a number of other theories.

THE INTEGRATIVE DEVELOPMENT OF SUBSTANTIVE NEW THEORIES OF PSYCHOTHERAPY: METHODS

There are two ways of integrating therapies into a single overall integrative theory of psychotherapy. One is to start with therapies that share the same parent theory of human beings. These therapies can be organized into a single integrative theory of psychotherapy. The second way is to start with a significantly modified theory of human beings. Once you accomplish that, you can develop a theory of psychotherapy that integrates those therapies that now properly fall under your significantly modified theory of human beings.

Notice that the key to both ways lies in the theory of human beings. Do something constructive with the theory of human beings, and the way is clear to the integrative development of new theories of psychotherapy.

I know that many therapists are eager to integrate therapies; there is a great deal of fervency and noise. The trouble is that we have not found ways of doing this. In this section I will first describe some ways that are being tried, but which I regard as essentially unworkable. Then I will turn to the two ways which I do regard as workable. I too have faith in our developing theories of psychotherapy that integrate families of our many current therapies. But there are ways that will work and there are ways that are best abandoned.

Generally unworkable methods

Most clinical theorists who are concerned with the integrative development of new theories of psychotherapy agree that this cannot be done by trying to put together several different theories of human beings (Franks, 1984; Franks & Wilson, 1979; Goldfried, 1980, 1982b; Krasner, 1978). Almost by definition, a social learning theory of human beings differs in fundamental ways from an existential-humanistic theory of human beings and from a psychoanalytic one. They cannot retain their fundamentally separate characters and still fit together in some integrative way. It is little wonder that so many theorists agree on the general fruitlessness of such an attempt. Remember, this is not even an attempt to integrate different theories of human beings to produce a new one, but merely to put them together in some way that they can coexist. It cannot be done. You cannot integrate therapies having different parent theories of human beings.

A therapist may try to put together five or six therapies that have five or six different sets of conceptions of human beings.

The resultant mix talks about the biological foundations of human behavior, considers growth and development in terms of Piaget, Freud, and Erikson, with a dash of social learning theory, highlights language, thought, and cognition with contributions by Bruner, Brown, and Chomsky, and thinks of personality in terms of Adler, Maslow, Kelly, with a little Freud and Angyal. They do not mix well, and they certainly do not integate smoothly. It is simply not feasible to try and develop a new integrative theory of psychotherapy by assembling a loose mixture of theories of human beings from pieces that are distinctive and cannot combine together. Yet some claimants to new theories of psychotherapy rather cavalierly refer to a theory of human beings containing a little of Bruner, Freud, Angyal, Adler, Chomsky, Piaget, and others. It is infeasible to try to develop a new integrative theory of psychotherapy by assembling a loose package of poor fitting parts of various theories of human beings. This is one generally unworkable approach.

Some therapists discover a concrete operation that is taken as part of some other approach, adopt that concrete operation, and proclaim that they developed a new theory of psychotherapy which integrates the two theories. For example, a psychodynamic therapist goes to a series of workshops and is taken with three concrete procedures. One workshop includes the use of a simple reassuring patting of the patient's shoulder when she is hurting, a gentle touch. A second workshop includes the presenter's telling a patient to say it again with more feeling. In the third workshop, the presenter uses a lot of good reflections. All three concrete procedures are appealing to the therapist, and are not part of what she ordinarily does. She adopts them and likes using them. She writes about her way of doing therapy, and says that she has developed a new theory of psychotherapy that integrates psychodynamic, humanistic (gentle touching of the patient's shoulder), Gestalt (telling the patient to say it again with feeling), and client-centered (reflections). Here is a second way of trying to develop an integrative theory of psychotherapy that will not work.

I draw a sharp distinction between concrete procedures and a theory of psychotherapy (cf. Figure 1). A therapist may start patting a patient on the shoulder without necessarily modifying the theory of psychotherapy. A therapist may adopt the use of reflections without taking on some alien theory of psychotherapy. At the level of concrete procedures, one may make all sorts of changes without integrating a theory of psychotherapy with another. Also, I consider that no theory of psychotherapy has exclusive rights over any concrete procedure. I can tell a patient to say it again with more feeling without my thereby integrating my current theory with that of Gestalt. If I follow a psychodynamic theory, I can use a simple reflection without being client-centered. No therapy *owns* a reassuring pat on the shoulder. In general, it is unworkable to try and develop an integrative theory of psychotherapy by adding a few concrete procedures, even if those concrete procedures are typically associated with some other theory. This is a second way that does not work.

There is a third way of trying to integrate theories of psychotherapy. It consists of adding a component or two from some other therapies, and thereby considering that you have developed a new theory that integrates them all. Indeed, it is common to assert that we have developed an integrative new theory by combining components from a number of different therapies. One therapist combines a few Gestalt and bioenergetic stratagems with a client-centered relationship and a psychodynamic mode of describing patients. Another therapist combines a psychoanalytic mode of listening-observing with principles of change involving both experiencing and insight-understanding, and adds a few therapeutic stratagems taken from cognitive behavior theory. These therapists generally regard the product as the integrative development of a new theory of psychotherapy. I do not agree.

I submit that such combining of components can be done *only* when the several contributions come from therapies sharing the same parental theory of human beings.

Consider trying to integrate systematic desensitization into psychoanalytic therapy, and thereby developing a new integrative therapy. My thesis is that this cannot be done—unless there is a significant change in the psychoanalytic theory of human beings. As long as the therapist accepts the psychoanalytic theory of human beings, the new component must be rejected as unsuitable. Let us apply the four ways of judging the supposed new theory of psychotherapy discussed earlier.

The first criterion is that the new theory is to have a reasonably high goodness-of-fit with the parent theory of human beings. I cannot see how the conceptual foundation of systematic desensitization can groove well into a psychoanalytic theory of human beings. There may be some psychoanalytic therapists, very much attracted to systematic desensitization, who are trying to fit it into the psychoanalytic theory of human beings, but I have yet to come across such an achievement.

Secondly, the new theory is to provide a clear statement of its components, including the integrated one. I believe this can be done. There can be a clear statement of systematic desensitization. However, the third criterion poses a real problem. Adding the therapeutic stratagem of systematic desensitization will have powerful ripple effects on all the other components of the old psychoanalytic theory of psychotherapy, and the direction will indeed be toward the development of a wholesale new theory of psychotherapy. But this is countered by a virtual impossibility of changing these other components while maintaining the psychoanalytic theory of human beings. Consider the requisite changes in the higher-order description of patients and also the changes in the therapeutic goals which would have to occur by adding systematic desensitization—changes which cannot be made while retaining the psychoanalytic theory of human beings.

The final criterion also poses a serious problem. I find it virtually impossible to integrate systematic desensitization into a modified psychoanalytic theory of psychotherapy in such a way as to meet the conditions-operations-consequences criterion. The new theory would have to identify the psychoanalytic conditions under which systematic desensitization is called for, and to show that these are the psychoanalytic consequences of using systematic desensitization. That would be a remarkable accomplishment. For example, in order to introduce systematic desensitization at this point in the session, the therapist would have to have some new way of identifying the proper "condition." That calls for a substantially modified way of listening to what the patient says and of framing higher-order descriptions of the patient. In order to do this, however, the psychoanalytic theory of human beings would have to be substantially altered to accommodate the conceptual foundations which yield a way of listening and a way of describing patients that is cordial to systematic desensitization.

Wherever we start, we run into the same barrier: that is, you cannot integrate systematic desensitization into a psychoanalytic therapy *without substantially modifying* the psychoanalytic theory of human beings.

I suggest that this third way will not work. It is not feasible to try to integrate components from several therapies. It cannot be done by adding a few components to some core therapy. It cannot be done by combining components from several therapies in order to develop some supposed new therapy that integrates them all. None of this can be done without substantially modifying the parent theory of human beings.

Here are three ways of trying to develop a new theory of psychotherapy that integrates several therapies. None of these ways are workable. They may have laudable aims, but they are not feasible no matter how hard we try. Let us now turn to two ways that I believe *are* workable.

Integrative development of theories of psychotherapy that share the same parent theory of human beings

The history of psychotherapy is one in which a number of different theories of practice have been generated out of the same overarching theory of human beings. Over the years, a family of psychotherapists may well share a somewhat similar theory of human beings, while their theories of psychotherapy go in rather different directions. For example, there are many different behavioral theories of psychotherapy. Since mid-century or so, practitioners who hold to much the same learning theory of what human beings are like, how they come about and how they behave, have produced substantially different behavioral therapies. The existential-humanistic theory of human beings lies behind many psychotherapies that differ from one another while sharing the same familial theory of human beings. From sensitivity groups to client-centered therapy, from phenomenological therapies to focusing, there are many therapies that claim allegiance to the existential-humanistic theory of human beings.

Within the psychoanalytic-psychodynamic theory of human beings, the same story holds. There is a more or less orthodox psychoanalytic theory of psychotherapy, a number of variant psychoanalytic schools, and a myriad of different psychodynamic-psychoanalytic theories of psychotherapy. Yet all of these share a familial allegiance to a single psychoanalytic theory of human beings with its ego and unconscious, its psychoanalytic stages of development, its repression and projection, neuroses and psychoses, and all the other characteristics.

Theories of human beings may be understood as rather loose bodies of thought or as rigorous systems of constructs. There are many ways to categorize these theories of human beings, and many ways to understand their relationships with theories of psychotherapy. Yet it seems clear to me that each of our big theories of human beings is related to a number of different psychotherapies, sometimes to a rather large number. When we shift over to the various psychotherapies that fall within the same general theory of human beings, I submit that there is plenty of room here for integration into a substantively new theory of psychotherapy. The proposition may be stated as follows: The integrative development of a substantive new theory of psychotherapy will occur *to the extent* that theories of psychotherapy share a common parental theory of human beings.

Indeed, I see this as a worthwhile and constructive enterprise. But it calls for a particular attitude toward family kinship. It calls for an acknowledgment that several psychotherapies really share a single overarching theory of human beings. It is always possible to emphasize *differences* in the larger theory of human beings, and these differences may be preserved and built up to prevent any real efforts at integration. Within the large psychoanalytic theory of human beings, there are always those who assert the differences between the object relations theory of human beings and the orthodox psychoanalytic theory, between Adlerian and Frommian and Horneyian theories of human beings. If, however, there is an emphasis upon the common shared theory of human beings, then the family of therapies will tend to integrate with one another into a smaller number of substantively new theories of psychotherapy.

There is a kind of natural process whereby therapies sharing the same theory of human beings invite integrative development. On this basis, implosive therapy leans toward counter-conditioning therapy rather than toward Gestalt therapy or transactional analysis. Rational-emotive therapy and cognitive therapy are more drawn toward one another than toward existential analysis or primal integration therapy. Accordingly, implosive therapy, counter-conditioning therapy, and a number of other therapies falling under a similar learning theory of human beings would tend to invite the integrative development of a substantive new theory of psychotherapy. For those who are drawn toward the integrative development of theories of psychotherapy, much of their work is already cut out for them when they start with theories of psychotherapy sharing a familial theory.

But what about some examples? Is there a major new psychoanalytic theory of psychotherapy that integrates most of the family members? What about a major existential-humanistic or learning approach that does the integrative job? If this is a feasible way of undertaking this first strategy, where are the products?

I believe that we have no good examples, as yet. But I also believe they are coming, and that this is one avenue along which they will develop. One of the reasons for the lack of major good examples is that much of the energies of integrationists have been dedicated toward the other strategies—so far. Another reason is that it takes *time* to integrate theories of psychotherapy, even those that share the same parental theory of human beings. It has only been in the latter half of this century that the various behavior therapies bloomed. Only recently have many set to work trying to integrate the various therapies, which will take time. But this is one way of going about this enterprise. It can work.

The formulation of a modified theory of human beings

Change a theory of human beings, and there will be corresponding changes in theories of psychotherapy. For those who are concerned with integrating psychotherapies, the most promising gateway is a significantly modified theory of human beings. Indeed, once a significant change occurs in a theory of human beings, the exciting challenge lies in the implications for the integrative development of substantive new theories of psychotherapy.

The psychoanalytic theory of human beings has undergone a number of significant changes which essentially comprise a modified theory of human beings. I shall cite two. One is the impact of the ego object relations theorists, notably Fairbairn, Horner, Kernberg, Mahler, Kohut, Guntrip, Hartmann, Klein, Winnicott, and others. A second is through the work of existentialial psychoanalytic theorists such as Ellenberger, May, Binswanger, Wyss, Farber, Gurwitsch, and others. I believe that each of these reformulations of a psychoanalytic theory of human beings has the potential for yielding quite new theories of psychotherapy capable of integrating a number of current theories of psychotherapy. Although both of these reconceptualizations have been around for many decades, the integrative development of substantive new theories of psychotherapy has yet to occur. But the potential is there. Sooner or later there will be a substantial object relations psychoanalytic theory of human beings and a substantial existential psychoanalytic theory of human beings. Once they have form and shape, they will provide the integrative superstructure for a new theory of psychotherapy that brings together many of our current therapies into each of these two new families.

But these are only big projects waiting on the drawing board. In refreshing contrast, I believe it is the work of Wachtel (1977, 1978, 1981, 1982a, 1982b, 1984) that exemplifies how the significant modification of a psychoanalytic theory of human beings has opened the way to the integrative development of a new theory of psychotherapy which blends components from psychoanalytic, psychodynamic, and behavioral theories of psychotherapy. In a significant reformulation of the psychoanalytic theory of human beings, Wachtel has essentially set aside the psychoanalytic libido, departed from the psychoanalytic topographical structure of personality, and has added such major new features as a distinctive way of conceptualizing problems and pathological behavioral states ("cyclical psychodynamics"), together with other modifications which effectively constitute a substantially modified theory of human beings. Armed with this new theory of human beings, Wachtel is thereby led to the integrative blending of psychoanalytic, psychodynamic, and behavioral theories of psychotherapy. It is a masterful piece of work exemplifying the construction of a new integrative theory of psychotherapy through the gateway of a new theory of human beings. Here is one live example of how to carry out this first strategy for integrating psychotherapies.

My own efforts toward developing an integrative theory of psychotherapy started with no discernible way of doing therapy or theory of human beings. Yet I was intrigued with both. Psychotherapy was absolutely fascinating to me, and notions about what human beings were like attracted me mainly because I sensed such notions had some kind of connection with whatever I was doing in psychotherapy. Indeed, I had no theory of psychotherapy, not even a loose collection of ideas about psychotherapy. Increasingly I turned to the literature on the theories of human beings to put a semblance of order on whatever I was doing as a psychotherapist. I was especially drawn toward the writings of psychotherapists. They seemed concerned with the questions I faced as a psychotherapist. I wasn't ready to figure out how to do psychotherapy. I was just unable to answer questions about how my patients got that way, why they would make their lives so miserable, how come some had strange and hurtful conditions in their bodies while others did not, and quantities of other questions about human beings rather than psychotherapy.

Mainly, I turned to the existential-humanistic literature because it was attractive to me and because readings in the other ways of making sense of human beings left me unsettled. Here is where the problems arose. A little of what I was reading made exciting sense of what I should be doing in psychotherapy.

However, most of the philosophical literature left me even more confused. But some of what I *did* grasp in the whole vast body of writings of the existential and humanistic theorists—Husserl, Camus, Jaspers, Heidegger, Nietzsche, and Sartre—provided the beginnings of an organized sense of what to do as a psychotherapist. But with even more, I found myself *not* agreeing, and I still had no answers to too many questions about the human beings who were my patients.

My solution was to frame out a theory of human beings that was rooted in some of the existential-humanistic conceptions, grew to be different in many respects, and with added pieces here and there on issues that I found missing in that literature (Mahrer, in press). The venture culminated in a significantly modified existential-humanistic theory of human beings for psychotherapists (Mahrer, 1978a). For example, its theory of how infants were developed, how the basic stuff of personality was originated, and the stages and plateaus of human development were quite apart from those of existential theorists and the main body of humanistic theorists represented by Maslow, Buhler, and others (Thomas, 1985). It began with a new reading, a modified theory of human beings from the existential-humanistic body of writings.

Once I had a way of making sense of my patients and what was there inside them and outside them, it was easy to decline whole chunks of psychotherapeutic writings and to embrace others. In other words, once I was reasonably clear on a parental theory of human beings, I could connect with the rich literature on psychotherapy. Developing an integrated theory of psychotherapy meant borrowing bits and pieces from lots of different theories of psychotherapy both inside and outside of the existential-humanistic therapies. My trusted framework was my theory of human beings, and this allowed me to assemble and to organize a theory of psychotherapy out of what was already available in many of the therapies that were around. At one end was the modified existential-humanistic theory of human beings. At the other end was the tough laboratory of actual psychotherapeutic work, seeing what seemed to work and what did not. In between was the developing experiential theory of psychotherapy (Mahrer, 1983a, 1986a).

Here, then, are two examples of integrating psychotherapies by formulating a modified theory of human beings. There are other examples. The message they all provide is that the integrative development of substantive new theories of psychotherapy proceeds through the gateway of theories of human beings. One method is to integrate theories of psychotherapy that share the same parent theory of human beings. A second method is to formulate a modified theory of human beings that allows for the integrative development of a substantive new theory of psychotherapy. Both methods work, and both proceed through the gateway of theories of human beings. This is the first strategy in the integration of psychotherapy.

CONSEQUENCES FOR THE FIELD OF PSYCHOTHERAPY

Suppose that there were a concerted movement to integrate the various psychotherapies by means of this first strategy. Suppose that there were efforts to develop substantive new theories of psychotherapy that sought to integrate a number of psychotherapies falling under a single parent theory of human beings. And suppose that there were other efforts to formulate modified theories of human beings, and thereby to develop new theories of psychotherapy aimed at integrating a number of others extant. If these movements were to proceed, what are the likely consequences for the field of psychotherapy?

There will be increased study of the formal properties of theories of psychotherapy. At present, we are rather hesitant to refer to "theories of psychotherapy." We easily refer to theories of cognition, theories of motivation, theories of learning, sensation, memory, psychological development, personality. With regard to psychotherapy, however, we more easily speak of approaches or schools or even systems, but not theories. One of the reasons is that when it comes to the psychotherapies we are rather skimpy on actual theory. If you exclude statements that more properly belong to theories of human beings, and also statements that refer to concretely specific operating procedures, there is precious little left to present as our theories of psychotherapy.

If, however, this first strategy catches hold, one of the consequences will be increased study of the formal properties of theories of psychotherapy. We have a fair literature on the study of the formal properties of our other theories. Philosophers of science even mention our theories of personality and our theories of learning, and there are ways of assessing their formal properties, showing the ways of gauging their rigor against recognized criteria of theoretical systems. As this first strategy is followed there will develop a study of the formal properties of our theories of psychotherapy as sheer theories. It will be encouraged by those who are at work trying to develop substantive new theories of psychotherapy.

I have proposed seven components of a theory of psychotherapy. My impression is that this is little more than a sophomoric first approximation, and that we will soon have much more rigorously sophisticated lists of the formal components of theories of psychotherapy. Along with this will come comparative analyses of the current theories based upon formal study of these theories *as* theories. Which theories are incomplete? How do they compare with one another as sheer theoretical *structures*? Where are the formal problems in a Freudian theory of psychoanalysis, an experiential or a client-centered theory of psychotherapy? Given any theory of psychotherapy, what is the profiling of its strengths and weaknesses? We will be able to ask and to answer these questions with increased study of the formal properties of theories of psychotherapy, and this will become a respectable area of study.

There will be a gradual evolution toward integration of theories of psychotherapy. Psychotherapies that share the same parental theory of human beings will sooner or later integrate with one another. The framework *is there*. It may take some time, but there will be a gradual evolution toward integration. It does not matter whether there is a modified theory of human beings that provides the integrative framework, or whether a number of current therapies already share a single parental theory of human beings. Gradually an overarching single theory of psychotherapy will evolve, and that will be the integrative glue for the development of *families* of psychotherapy.

This will not occur because of a sense of family kinship or loyalty or belonging. It is a matter of the foundation for each of the components that comprise a theory of psychotherapy. Because so many behavioral theories share the same general learning theory of human beings, there is a fundamental integrative pull from each of the components. Each behavioral therapy will be pulled to elicit similar kinds of useful material. They will tend to share one another's way of listening /observing. They have a basis for exchanging therapeutic goals. They can adopt one another's therapeutic stratagems. The presence of a shared parental theory of human beings means that the various behavior therapies will tend to move gradually toward a natural integration. As long as there is a shared parental theory of human beings, there will be a gradual evolution toward integration, whether the shared theory of human beings already *exists,* or whether it occurs as a *newly modified* theory of human beings comes about.

Psychotherapists will also be personality theorists. The traditional role of the psychotherapist is that of the professional who plies the trade of psychotherapy. They are practitioners who have mastered their craft. If, however, this first strategy catches hold, practitioners will be much more familiar with their chosen theory of psychotherapy and thereby to their underlying theories of human beings. I foresee that a larger proportion of practitioners will be much more familiar with the theories of human beings upon which their practice is based. This first strategy means that psychotherapists will be more conversant with *why* they do what they do, and that means that psychotherapists will also be *personality theorists.* This first strategy says that the golden gateway is the theory of human beings, the theory of personality. The consequence is that a larger proportion of practitioners will be comfortable playing with the stuff of personality theory.

There will be fewer and better theories of psychotherapy. One of the fondest hopes of the integrationists is that there will be *fewer* schools and approaches to psychotherapy. This first strategy will, I believe, be one way of realizing these hopes. There will be a reduction in the sheer number of psychotherapies as there is increasing integration among those that share the same parent theory of human beings. Even as new theories of human beings develop, the consequence will tend to be a reduction in the sheer number of psychotherapies as these new theories of human beings promote more encompassing theories of psychotherapy. The net result will tend to be a convergent reduction in the sheer number of psychotherapies.

I expect that the ceiling will be the number of genuinely different theories of human beings. Accordingly, I foresee the direction of change as toward somewhere between five and ten genuinely different theories of psychotherapy, each connected to its own genuinely different theory of human beings.

One of the current trends is toward the proliferation of specialty therapies. We are seeing special therapeutic programs for patients described as needing assertiveness training, career counseling, family problem resolution, reduction of work-related stress, and so on. I believe that the impact of this first strategy will be toward a smaller number of psychotherapies that are more comprehensive. Specialty programs will be encompassed within larger and more comprehensive approaches. I see, for example, behavior therapists whose specialty may be that of working with learning difficulties in children or working with gynecological patients in hospitals, but their theory of psychotherapy will be a shared behavioral therapy. All in all, the direction of increased comprehensiveness can and will accommodate specialty programs.

At the same time, I foresee that this first strategy will evolve therapies that are better in the sense of being more rigorous, more conceptually sound, more tied to actual theory.

These are the consequences of pursuing this first strategy of integrating psychotherapies. I like these consequences, and believe they are good for the field of psychotherapy. When we think of the integration of psychotherapies, this is one of the strategies. But it is only one.

Chapter 2

THE INTEGRATION OF CONCRETELY SPECIFIC OPERATING PROCEDURES

There is a second meaning and strategy of integrating psychotherapies. Unlike the first strategy, it does not involve the development of a new theory of psychotherapy. In fact, it is almost at the other extreme. If you arrange the six strategies in terms of where they fit into Figure 1, the first strategy is at the top, starts with theories of human beings, and deals with the development of a new theory of psychotherapy. The second strategy is at the other end of Figure 1. It consists essentially of adopting or borrowing some of the concretely specific operating procedures from other approaches.

CONCRETELY SPECIFIC OPERATING PROCEDURES VERSUS THERAPEUTIC STRATAGEMS

As indicated in Figure 1, one of the components of a theory of psychotherapy is a general therapeutic stratagem. This refers to a general tactic or program that therapists carry out. It includes such stratagems as relaxation training, transference analysis, social awareness training, cognitive problem-solving, dream analysis, and so on. Just about everything the therapist does can be included in some larger therapeutic stratagem. At that level, we can describe what the therapist is doing now as relaxation training, and, later, the therapist is doing cognitive problem-solving. We can follow the therapist statements and describe the kind of general stratagem that is being carried out. That is one level of description.

But there is another level of description much closer to the actual words in each therapist statement. If the level of description for therapeutic stratagems is regarded as "molar," then there is a level of description which is called "molecular." We are looking at the same therapist statement, but now we are describing something closer to nuts and bolts, to the concretely specific operating procedures. Each therapeutic stratagem is comprised of many operating procedures, and some operating procedures are found in several therapeutic stratagems. The terms "therapeutic stratagem" and "operating procedures" are not as important as recognizing that there is a significant difference between the larger tactics and programs that therapists carry out (therapeutic stratagems) and the concretely specific nuts and bolts operating procedures. This distinction is crucial for the second strategy.

Here are four statements that many therapists may say in the course of carrying out some larger therapeutic stratagem:

T: It would feel wonderful if you could show some anger without getting so much tension.

T: The big man in the dream, the man who has other patients milling around in his office and doesn't give you all the time that you deserve. What do you make of him?

T: So call him a jerk again. Go ahead. Say it louder.

T: Tell me when these sleeping problems first began, all you can remember about what was happening then, in your life.

If we describe what the therapist is doing in each of the four statements, at the level of concretely specific operating procedures, we may say that the therapist is reflecting or restating the patient's feeling, inviting the patient's association or interpretation of a dream element, instructing the patient to say it again with more feeling, obtaining background information on the problem. These are operating procedures.

One of the characteristics of operating procedures is that

they bear implications on what the patient is to do next (Mahrer, 1985; Mahrer, Clark, Comeau, & Brunette, in press). That is, each operating procedure contains an invitation or instruction or prescription for what the patient is to do in the next statement or so. Put yourself in the role of the patient. If a therapist said, "Tell me when these sleeping problems first began, all you can remember about what was happening then, in your life," you would probably sense a pull for you to say something like, "Well, it started when I found out that I was pregnant, and that's when I started waking up in the middle of the night and couldn't get back to sleep." Each operating procedure is geared toward eliciting some kind of response from the patient. This is not a characteristic of general therapeutic stratagems, but it is a characteristic of operating procedures.

A therapeutic stratagem is comprised of many concrete and specific operating procedures. If a therapist in training is told to do assertion training or dream analysis, the therapist can go ahead and do it provided that he or she knows what to do. The "what to do" refers to the operating procedures. Two therapists can be engaged in dream analysis, but they will be doing quite different things if one uses operating procedures laid down by Freud, and the other uses operating procedures from Jung or Boss. Therapeutic stratagems are components of a theory of psychotherapy. They relate to the actual statements of the therapist only in a general way. In contrast, operating procedures refer to the actual statements that the therapist carries out. They are the working nuts and bolts of the therapeutic stratagems.

Here are some operating procedures: clarifying the role of patient, providing information on therapeutic arrangements, telling the patient how to focus attention, suggesting-advising a given extratherapy change in behavior, inviting the patient to express it with more feeling, drawing the patient's attention to the therapist-patient relationship, asking the patient to give her reaction to what the therapist just said, obtaining demographic information, disputing the patient's idea or belief, synthesizing the theme in what the patient has been saying, drawing the patient's attention to an immediate change in topic, putting into words what the patient seems to be meaning, revealing something personal about the therapist, sharing in the patient's laughter, suggesting a causal pattern from the historical material, encouraging the patient in the proposed change. There are scores and scores more. Yet each of these refers to a specific operation or act the therapist does, and each one is aimed at trying to get the patient to *do* something, to *be* some way, to *respond* in some way that is *built into* that concretely specific operating procedure.

Figure 2 provides an illustration of the difference between the therapeutic stratagems and operating procedures in experiential psychotherapy. The four boxes are the therapeutic stratagems. They are numbered because they are to occur in that phased sequence in each session. Above each of the four therapeutic stratagems are the classes of operating procedures that are used in implementing each of the therapeutic stratagems. For example, each session begins with the therapeutic stratagem of attaining a level of strong feeling. One class of operating procedures for attaining this level of strong feeling includes procedures whereby the patient is invited to let the feeling show and grow. The patient is shown how to allow this feeling to occur, to happen more, to grow. Any feeling is welcomed as long as it is here now. Accordingly, the patient is shown how to allow herself to feel confused and bewildered, or silly and giddy, or anxious and tense, or defiant and rebellious, or whining and tearful, or whatever feeling may be present right now. In the same way, sets of specific operating procedures comprise each class of operating procedures above each of the four therapeutic stratagems given in Figure 2.

The Meaning of Integrating Psychotherapies at the Level of Concretely Specific Operating Procedures

This second integrative strategy occurs when one therapy borrows or uses a working procedure from some other therapy, or when two or more therapies share the same operating procedures. In general, this second strategy occurs quietly. There is little fanfare when a Sullivanian psychoanalyst adopts a working procedure that is generally associated with experiential psychotherapy, or when client-centered and behavioral therapists

Opening guideline instructions
Enabling feeling to become at least moderate
    Accept any new feeling and attentional center
    Guess at nature of feeling
    Let feeling show and grow (use specific methods)
    Make feelinged attentional center-scene alive and real (use
        specific methods)
    Emphasize readiness and willingness
Going from moderate to strong level of feeling
    • Describe strong level • Describe behaviors • Emphasize
    choice
    1. ATTAINING THE LEVEL OF STRONG FEELING

↓

Listen for the experiencing
Welcome-accept the experiencing
Describe the experiencing
Lift out and express the experiencing
    2. APPRECIATING THE EXPERIENCING

↓

Guideline instructions for locating earlier scene
Identify earlier scene by means of experiencing or situational
    context
Guideline instructions for being experiencing in earlier scene
Pt. is being the experiencing in earlier scene (T joins in)
    3. BEING THE EXPERIENCING IN EARLIER SCENE

↓

Select:
    Mode of undergoing being-behavior change
    Prospective situation-scene
    Behavior
    Rehearsal for reality
    Behavioral commitment
    4. NEW WAYS OF BEING-BEHAVING IN PROSPECTIVE
        SCENES

**Figure 2.   Therapeutic Stratagems and Classes of Operating
Procedures in Each Session of Experiential Psychotherapy.**

share quite similar operating procedures. Of course, you will not be able to notice this second strategy unless you see videotapes or listen to audiotapes or read verbatim transcripts of actual sessions. Sometimes this second strategy is given a label. For example, Goldstein and Stein (1976), Lazarus (1967), and London (1964) refer to this as "technical eclecticism," meaning that any approach is free to be eclectic in borrowing the operating procedures or techniques of other approaches at this concrete and specific level of actual work (cf. Gendlin, 1986).

The popularity of this second strategy is hinted at in the wealth of process research that studies the distribution of specific working operations across the various therapeutic approaches. Lots of specific operations are found in lots of therapies. Clinical researchers say that therapies freely use each others' specific procedures, and they identify this strategy as widespread (Bergin & Lambert, 1978; Sloane, Staples, Cristol, Yorkston, & Whipple, 1975). Grinker (1976) even suggests that psychoanalytic therapists tend to borrow and use working operations from other therapies far removed from psychoanalysis.

This strategy rests upon at least three propositions that allow so many therapies to share so many operating procedures. Each of these propositions is explicitly or, more typically, *implicitly* accepted by those who use this strategy.

There is a rich pool of concretely specific operating procedures. As indicated in Figure 1, there are theories of psychotherapy and, quite separate from these theories, there is a pool of operating procedures. Those who follow this second strategy accept the proposition that there is such a pool of operating procedures, and that the pool is independent of any particular theory of psychotherapy.

But just how rich is this common pool and what are its specific constituents? What are these common operating procedures? In order to follow this strategy it would be helpful to have answers to these questions, but as yet we have none. This would seem to be the job of clinical researchers, yet they have only tackled the job from the side. That is, clinical researchers have been more concerned with assembling a set of categories of more or less common operating procedures than with identifying a comprehensive list of operating procedures. Yet clinical researchers have been active in compiling category systems of the relatively common operating procedures. Reviews indicate that we have two or three dozen such category systems (Elliott, Stiles, Shiffman, Barker, Burstein, & Goodman, 1982; Goodman & Dooley, 1976; Hill, 1983; Russell & Stiles, 1979). Most of these systems include 8 to 15 mutually exclusive categories which are relatively common across approaches. My own category system (Mahrer, 1983c) was expressly designed to include operating procedures from the major psychotherapies such as client-centered, psychodynamic, analytic, experiential, behavioral and rational-emotive. It includes 35 mutually exclusive operating procedures. In general, it is my impression that a careful study would yield somewhere between 50 and 100 different operating procedures.

The pool of operating procedures is public, not private. This rich pool of operating procedures is part of the public marketplace. Any therapist, regardless of approach, can obtain operating procedures from this public pool. No therapeutic approach has exclusive rights of ownership over any of these operating procedures.

There is a serious side to this matter of public versus private ownership. Some therapies might well want their operating procedures to be exclusively owned by their approach. They insist that they are the ones who developed the operating procedure, that the operation is characteristic of the given approach, and that other approaches should not even consider using the operation without training in the host approach. While there may be a few operating procedures that are so regarded by most therapies, integrationists do not accept the rights of private ownership. I am with the integrationists here. Every operating procedure is a part of the public marketplace, and may be adopted by any therapy at all.

Obviously some approaches will have no use for operations that are essential to other approaches. I doubt if a cognitive behavioral therapy would regard free association as essential. Nor would most psychoanalytic approaches find a solid use for an operation in which the patient is instructed to "be" a license plate, or a quivering lip, or a runaway bus. But all of these operations are part of the public domain, and therapies are free to take whatever they find useful.

It is also obvious that some operations have been developed and refined by a given approach. Free association is largely from psychoanalytic therapy. Reflections are generally from client-centered therapy. Disputing irrational beliefs is mainly from rational-emotive therapy. Many operations have been produced by a particular approach, but once produced, it is now just another part of the public marketplace, to be used by any therapy whatsoever.

As indicated in Figure 1, a psychotherapy consists of the various components of the theory of that therapy. Client-centered therapy consists of its own version of each of the seven components. It does not consist of a mere collection of client-centered operating procedures. Indeed, many of the operating procedures may be replaced with more useful ones, and client-centered therapy would still be client-centered therapy. If psychoanalysis is identified with the various *components* of a psychoanalytic theory of psychotherapy, it will develop. The more psychoanalysis is identified with and limited to particular *operating procedures,* the more is that therapy atrophying itself. I see no reason why any therapy has to be restricted to its present array of concretely specific operating procedures. There may always be a few useful operations in the public pool, and therapies are enriched and developed by always shopping for better and more useful operations. The public marketplace is a wonderful place to shop.

It must be understood that these operations are concrete and specific. They are functional and operational. "Interpretation" is a large, loose, and lumpy category. When we get down to the level of specific operating procedures, there are several working kinds of interpretation. Even within the several psychoanalytic schools there are Freudian interpretations, Rankian, Adlerian, object relations interpretations, and so on. Then there are therapist *operations,* which seem remarkably *like* interpretations when client-centered reflections get ambitious and go deeper. But there are also distinctive rational-emotive interpretations that are substantially different from the commonplace kind, and Jungian interpretations are another unique story. All in all, there are lots of different operating procedures at the concretely specific working level of study, and all of these are contained in the public pool of these operations.

Each therapy can shop from the public marketplace of operating procedures. Therapists who use this second integrative strategy believe that their therapy can profit from wise shopping at the public marketplace. There will always be new technology, and there is always the possibility that some new operating procedures can improve the therapy. Experiential therapists have a set of explicit jobs that must be carried out by each set of operating procedures. These jobs are assigned by the theory of experiential psychotherapy; but there is always room for better and more useful operating procedures. And this is the attitude of those who follow the second strategy. Restricting oneself to a current package of operating procedures is rather self-defeating. It is much more profitable to adopt and adapt specific procedures that are available publically. Therapies that use this second strategy regard their current set of procedures as expendable and as easily replaceable by better ones. On the other hand, therapies that seek to institutionalize their operating procedures will perhaps gain the sense of being a cult or an exclusive club or a secret fellowship, but this will be obtained at the expense of not having the therapy grow and develop. What is more, there will always be alien therapists and therapies who will pirate the protected operating procedures because most other approaches do not recognize exclusivity.

Those who follow the second integrative strategy believe that there are lots of concretely specific operating procedures that therapists carry out. They believe that this rich pool of operating procedures is, and should be, public rather than private, and they believe that their therapy and other therapies can profit by wise shopping from this public marketplace. Not all therapists share these beliefs. But those who do can carry out the second integrative strategy. They will turn to other therapies and therapists to look for and to adopt fresh and useful operating procedures, and thereby carry out the second strategy. We now turn to two ways of doing this second strategy.

HOW TO INTEGRATE PSYCHOTHERAPIES BY MEANS OF CONCRETELY SPECIFIC OPERATING PROCEDURES

There is a problem in carrying out this strategy. If you are going to add an operating procedure that is used by some other therapist, you have to have access to what other therapists actually do—to observe or listen to some other therapist doing psychotherapy. In our profession this is a pitiably rare occurrence. Dentists can see other dentists at work, physicians can watch other physicians. Lawyers can observe other lawyers. The same is true of cooks, truck drivers, engineers, architects, artists, dancers, physicists, mathematicians, and practitioners of most other trades and professions. But few psychotherapists ever get to watch and study the work of other psychotherapists. Even in our training, it is rare that trainees accrue 500 hours, or 50, or even 10 hours actually observing the ongoing work of genuine therapists doing therapy. Once a therapist graduates and is licensed, whole careers are spent without seeing and listening to other therapists whose actual operating procedures you just might adopt.

Of course there are exceptions. Some tapes are available of real therapists doing therapy. Some therapists put on workshops and demonstrations, although that is different from actually seeing their real work with patients. Some approaches are open to taping and verbatim transcripts. But most other approaches, especially psychoanalytic and Jungian, are explicit in not having full transcripts of sessions, in not having videotapes or audiotapes. In general, our field is exceptional in hiding the actual operating procedures that are carried out in our actual work. Ours is one of the few fields in which a person is to learn and to carry out the trade with tightly limited access to the actual work of colleagues.

Carrying out this second strategy requires that you study the actual work of other therapists. Some of these therapists are to be those whose approach is rather similar to your own. If you are a Gestalt therapist, then study the work of other Gestalt therapists. Carrying out this strategy also means that you study the work of therapists who fall outside your approach. I know how unwelcome this is. It is seldom that a therapist even has access to a verbatim transcript of a session or to a tape of a few sessions, from the work of another therapist. It is rare that therapists will study the actual operating procedures of other therapists close to their own school. It is almost unheard of for psychoanalytic therapists to study the verbatim work of a cognitive behavioral therapist, for therapists of one approach to spend hours studying the tapes of therapists from other approaches.

Yet this is precisely what you must do in order to carry out this second strategy: Watch other therapists doing actual therapy. Read verbatim transcripts of whole sessions. Observe videotapes of other therapists. Listen to audiotapes of the work of other therapists. Expose yourself to the concretely specific operating procedures of other therapists. See firsthand what your colleagues actually do.

Of all of these ways, my preference is listening to audiotapes. I have access to two wonderful sources. One is the tape library of the American Academy of Psychotherapists. Beginning its collection in the 1960s, the holdings include almost 200 tapes, many of which are of seasoned therapists conducting actual therapy sessions, and representing many different kinds of psychotherapies. The second source is my own collection which, over the past 30 years, has now grown to include 360 sessions conducted by about 50 therapists representing a rich diversity of approaches. Some of the therapists are exemplars, most of whom write a great deal about psychotherapy. But the precious balance is comprised of therapists who write little or nothing, and who merely ply their craft as fine masters of the art. I wrote to colleagues, inquired whom they and their acquaintances valued as fine therapists, and then pleaded with these special therapists to send me some of their tapes. Consequently I have a valuable library of tapes from lots of therapists, representing many psychotherapy-related professions and a range of therapeutic approaches. Whatever route you follow in gaining access to the actual observed or recorded work of therapists, this is the essential starting point in the strategy of integrating working operations.

The personal study of tapes

One way of carrying out this strategy is to listen to tapes. Listen by yourself or with a few others who are also intent on discovering new and effective therapeutic procedures. Do this on a more or less regular basis. I listen for about an hour or so every week or two, and have managed to accumulate at least 1000 hours of such tape listening over the past 30 years.

As you listen, pay especial attention to two events. One is when the therapist does something different from what you would ordinarily do right at this moment—and you are aware of a sense of arousal, keen interest, excitement, perhaps mixed with a dash of threat. Almost *everything* other therapists do is different from what you would do right here at this point in the session; and almost uniformly your reaction will be anything *but* aroused fascination. Yet there *will* be occasions when that therapist will depart from your way of dealing with that issue, and you will be keenly caught up. You and the therapist you are listening to are rolling along until the therapist says, "I really like you," or "Well, that's the dumbest thing I ever heard," or something that grabs your attention. Your reaction is split. That is not something you would do, and certainly not here. But also, there may be a sense of eagerness. What will the patient *do*? What will *happen*? So you listen, and now you are challenged, for even you have to admit that therapeutically new and desirable things are occurring. That therapist managed to achieve something you also would like to achieve, and now you have a problem. No one can force you to do what that therapist did, yet you have discovered something valuable, a crucial operating procedure. As you listen more, you are even more alert to surprises—operating procedures carried out by the therapist that *you* would never have tried. Sometimes the consequences justify what you yourself do and you therefore would not carry out the new operating procedure. But there are occasions when you are challenged to admit that the consequences of some of these new operating procedures are impressive, and you are drawn toward adoption. This is one way that the personal study of tapes pays off.

There is another way. It consists of your paying close attention to how the patient is *being* and what the patient is *doing*. Every so often will come a moment when you are struck that something remarkable is happening. The patient is being some way or doing something that you perceive as a solid evidence of progress, improvement, change. It may be that the patient is expressing an important insight, and such moments you recognize as vital. Or the patient had been agonizing in a heavy depression, and then it lifted, and the patient seems quite new and different, free of the persistent depression. Or, the continuous headache is suddenly gone. The continuously stuttering speech is now fluent. The ever-present fears or tightness or tormenting uncertainty have evaporated. You witness a thoroughly new personality, a radically different person. Here is a dramatic change in the behaviors, ways of being, or substantive personality.

You then work *backward,* by listening to what the therapist did, or what the therapist and patient together did. Maybe you listen to the last few interchanges, or maybe you listen to the last 5 or 10 minutes or more. As you listen, you begin to discover that the therapist did something that you do not usually do. In fact, you are introduced to a new operating procedure. If you want to bring about that moment of radical transformation, perhaps using that operating procedure will help. Here again is the challenge of adopting a new operating procedure.

By careful listening in these two ways, your attention will be focused upon a new and potentially effective operating procedure. The final step is completely up to you. If you are ready and willing to integrate that procedure into your own package, then you will be using the strategy of integrating concretely specific working operating procedures. But it must be stressed that the challenge and the opportunity lie with you and you alone.

Many years ago I listened to one tape graciously sent to me by a practitioner who did no publishing, and who certainly did not do experiential psychotherapy. It was the forty-third session with a man who was seen about three times a week. For a few initial minutes the patient gave the usual neutral, low-key material and then, quite suddenly, he started expressing strong feelings and impressively emotional material. He seemed to be talking directly to his brother, as if in a live interaction. I was amazed at how suddenly this patient was being and doing what I not only prized, but rarely achieved in my own sessions. How did the therapist get material that I wished I could get? I went back to the beginning of the session, just a few minutes earlier, and heard the therapist listening to the neutral opening for a minute or so. Then the therapist said, "OK, are you ready to begin? Lean back, close your eyes, and let the feelings fill you. Take all the time you need. Just let yourself feel whatever comes to you, and express whatever it is, good or bad, about anything at all. Let it start whenever you are ready." The patient paused for about 10 seconds, and then all that electrifying material just came pouring forth. I was excited and eager to try out that altogether new and *innocently* direct way of getting this matchless kind of therapeutic material. I therefore adopted that procedure.

When I began doing psychotherapy, I implicitly accepted two ideas about behavior change. One was that it will occur in its own proper time when the patient is ready. I should not *push*. Every so often I gently *encouraged*, but not frequently nor strongly. The second idea was that the behavior changes that were to occur were generally in relation to whatever seemed to be the patient's problem. Other kinds of behavior changes were ancillary or secondary to those in the vicinity of the patient's problem. Then a number of tapes by a number of fine therapists challenged those ideas. One therapist used methods somewhat akin to those of Eriksonian hypnotherapy. A second had his own brand of therapy, and a third relied mainly on a psychodynamic approach complemented and modified in her own distinctive way. At the end of nearly every session, these therapists were successful in enabling their patients to engage in a virtual explosion of all sorts of behavior changes as if therapy were a behavior-change popcorn machine. Some of the new behaviors related to what might be conceived as the patient's problem, while others seemed to come from other personality parts. The patients did all sorts of things with possible new ways of being and behaving. They sampled them, tried them out, added new ones, played with them, discarded some, rehearsed them, and generally revelled in new ways of being and behaving.

These therapists obtained in nearly every session far more behavior change than I obtained after weeks or months or much longer. I began to adopt their ideas about behavior change. Perhaps it could be obtained in virtually every session. Perhaps it could range far and wide, depending on what happened in that session. I studied the tapes of what these therapists did, how they managed to do it, and I tried to figure out the principles they used to engage in behavior change. Not all therapists may be as stimulated by what I heard. But for those who are ready, I submit that the personal study of tapes yields a wealth of possibilities for discovering and trying out new operating procedures.

The personal study of tapes is one way of integrating psychotherapies by means of concretely specific operating procedures. The clinician is discovering more about how to carry out a way of doing therapy, but one of the side effects is the integration of psychotherapies. As therapists venture further and further into studying the tapes of other therapists who do other kinds of therapy, and as these therapists borrow and use each others' operating procedures, they are using one version of the second integrative strategy.

It would be an advantage if there were a tape library explicitly designed for therapists who are ready and willing to discover and use other operating procedures; that is, to have a public pool of all of the operating procedures. Picture a large library of psychotherapy tapes organized around those moments that therapists like to see occurring in their sessions. If you prize rare moments of insight, then listen to designated tapes in order to discover new operating procedures for effecting such moments. That is a needed project. The second strategy calls for such a public library.

Clinical research on tapes: Discovery-oriented versus hypothesis-testing research. Another way of carrying out this second strategy follows the same general contours, but it has the added advantage of some research tools that can provide further rigor and exactitude to personal listening to tapes. Once again, we are looking for operating procedures that are useful and that can be integrated into therapeutic approaches.

Instead of listening to tapes by yourself or with a colleague, this method generally uses a *team* of judges, a psychotherapy research team. I prefer a rather large team of clinically sophisticated judges, practitioners who represent many different therapeutic approaches and who have some interest in clinical research (Mahrer, Paterson, Thériault, Roessler, & Quenneville, 1986). However, the size and composition of the research team is up to each researcher.

We listen to tapes of sessions conducted by therapists of all schools and approaches. Our aim is to locate moments when the patient is showing improvement, change, progress, movement. It is the same target as with the personal study of tapes; but we are assisted by a category system of all the good moments we could find by studying the psychotherapy research literature (Mahrer, 1985; Mahrer & Nadler, 1986). We had initially set out to compile this list by studying the clinical literature, but this task proved too overwhelming—although it remains to be done by someone. Instead, we chose to examine studies on psychotherapy, and to include in our categories all those moments that researchers deemed worthy of inclusion in their studies, regardless of outcome results, and findings. Accordingly, our list contains 12 categories taken from and representative of a large number of psychotherapeutic approaches. In abbreviated form, here is a description of each of the 12 categories:

1. *Providing meaningful material about personal self and/or interpersonal relations.* The client is providing (reporting, describing, expressing) material which is meaningful (useful, important, revealing, significant), and which pertains to the personal self and/or interpersonal relations.

2. *Describing-exploring the personal nature and meaning of feelings.* The client is engaging in bodily-felt, inner-focused description and exploration of the personal nature and meaning of immediate and ongoing feelings.

3. *Emerging of previously warded-off material.* The client is expressing significant material which had been previously warded off (defended against), and is now accompanied by strong positive or negative feelings.

4. *Expressing insight-understanding.* The client is expressing insight-understanding, accompanied by feelings of emotional arousal, indicative of a substantial change in the mode of seeing-construing oneself and the world, and bearing significant implications for the patient's well-being, personal and interpersonal behavior.

5. *Communicating expressively.* The client is communicating in a manner characterized by (a) a voice quality

which is active, alive, energetic, fresh, spontaneous, and vibrant; and/or (b) vividness and richness in the spoken words: figures of speech, colorful use of imagery and metaphor, strong sensual quality.

6. *Manifesting good working relationship with therapist.* The client's relationship with the therapist is characterized by high trust level, confidence in the helping intent of the therapist, valuing of the working alliance, active cooperation in the search for meaningful material, acceptance of substantive responsibility for effecting personal change.

7. *Expressing strong feelings toward therapist.* The client is expressing strong positive or negative feelings toward the therapist in an intensely personal relationship indicative of emotional bonding, confrontation, encounter, clash, or transference.

8. *Expressing strong feelings in extratherapy contexts.* The client is expressing strong feelings within the context of extratherapy scenes and situations which may be recent or remote, real or fantasied, personal or impersonal, internal or external.

9. *Manifesting a qualitatively altered personality state.* The client is manifesting (being, expressing) a qualitatively new and different personality state indicative of a radical shift or transformation in substantive personality.

10. *Undergoing new behaviors in imminent extratherapy world.* The client is undergoing (expressing, trying out) new ways of being and behaving within the imagined or fantasied imminent extratherapy world.

11. *Manifesting or reporting changes in target behaviors.* The client is manifesting or reporting the increased or decreased occurrence of behaviors (symptoms, thoughts, feelings) which have been targeted as change-markers.

12. *Expressing a general state of well-being.* The client is expressing (indicating, reporting) a general state of well-being characterized by relief, resolution of problems, satisfaction with oneself, happiness, good feelings, and positive well-being.

We provide each judge with a manual that includes a fuller description of each of these categories together with verbatim examples of each of the categories. It is important to understand that this list aims at including anything regarded as a good moment from the perspective of given therapeutic approaches. Accordingly, no therapy would likely welcome all 12 categories. Instead, each approach would lead toward a subset of the 12. For example, experiential psychotherapy accepts categories 7 to 10, and excludes the others as its good moments.

Each of the research members listens individually to tapes, complemented by the 12-fold category system and a verbatim transcript of the session. Since the judges are representative of various approaches, each judge initially is assigned those categories that are meaningful in that judge's approach. With a certain amount of balancing, each category is used by several judges. By going through the tape and the transcript this way, each patient statement is provisionally categorized by two or three judges or so, each using the categories that fit the judge's approach.

The next step is for the judges again to go through the tape and the transcript; only this time each judge agrees or disagrees with the provisional categorization obtained in the initial sweep. A criterion is used; for example, two-thirds of the total number of judges is to agree that a given patient statement falls into the category. If a particular judge is found to have a bias either for or against a particular category, that judge's ratings on that category may be weighted accordingly (Mahrer, Paterson, Thériault, Roessler, & Quenneville, 1986).

The result of all this work is a flagging of those patient statements that have been shown to represent instances of a particular category of good moment. It is even possible to distinguish between merely good instances of a given category and outstanding ones. In my own research work, I have my research team go through the tapes and transcripts a third time to identify these notable instances.

Next comes the exciting part. Having *located* these moments, the task is to study what preceded them to identify the precise operating procedures that led to them. We can study the immediately preceding therapist statements, and the penultimate therapist statements. We can go back as far as we wish, and we can study the operating procedures involving both therapist and patient. In any case, we discover operating procedures that are apparently instrumental in bringing about the favorable moments, and that is the payoff. Once these are discovered, we are again faced with the opportunity of *using* these operating procedures, especially those that provide the kinds of moments that we cherish in our own therapeutic work.

This kind of research aims at discovering new operating procedures that are instrumental in bringing about the in-session consequences we value. In effect, this kind of research yields inferences, hunches that can be framed as hypotheses for research that is designed to test the findings of this line of inquiry. I am drawing a distinction between "discovery-oriented" research and "hypothesis-testing" research. Looking for useful and effective operating procedures is discovery-oriented research. The aim is to find solutions, to look for answers to meaningful practical questions, to add to the body of clinical knowledge—to *discover* something. It has its own research philosophy, its own research methods and research designs. This kind of research is somewhat alien to traditional psychology. Discovery-oriented research does not rely on the standard and traditional research designs, methods, and procedures of psychology.

In contrast, most psychological research is geared toward hypothesis-testing, toward confirming or disconfirming some hypothesis that is its starting point. Such research is neither aimed toward discovery nor is it useful for discovery. It has limited use for finding solutions, looking for answers to meaningful practical questions, adding to the body of clinical knowledge, discovering things. Hypothesis-testing research is essentially unable to discover what operations effect what consequences under what conditions, although it is useful for confirming or disconfirming hypotheses generated by discovery-oriented research. Almost all of standard psychological research designs, methodologies, and procedures are limited to hypothesis-testing research. Not only are the findings from hypothesis-testing research of little or no use for discovery, that brand of research is unable to add to the body of clinical knowledge except to add or subtract an increment of confirmation or disconfirmation to the *current* body of knowledge. Accordingly, hypothesis-testing research has the effect of *reducing* the body of knowledge to that which can be held with higher degrees of confidence. If pieces of knowledge fail to gain confirmation, they are properly to be withdrawn from the body of knowledge. Thus the net result of hypothesis-testing research is to shrink the body of knowledge to that which can be held with reasonable levels of confidence.

This second strategy relies upon the designs, methodologies, and procedures of discovery-oriented research (Mahrer, 1976, 1979, 1985). For example, two studies followed this line of inquiry and emerged with interesting new ways of bringing about the categories of communicating expressively (category 5), expressing strong feelings in extratherapy contexts (category 8), undergoing new behaviors in the extratherapy world (category 10), expressing insight-understanding (category 4), and manifesting a qualitatively altered personality state (category 9) (Mahrer, Nadler, Gervaize, & Markow, 1986; Mahrer, Nadler, Dessaulles, & Gervaize, 1987). What is more, each of these studies found one set of operating procedures instrumental in bringing about these dramatic moments, and a second set of operating procedures that appeared to sustain and develop each of these moments. Here was a bonus from the research; for the therapists in each study not only brought about these good moments but also continued to sustain and develop them in ways which could now be framed as useful *hypotheses.*

A more focused use of this line of inquiry concentrates on a particular subcategory in one of the general categories. For example, some therapists value moments in which patients not only communicate expressively (category 5), but specifically do so by bursts of hearty laughter, as one subcategory of communicating expressively. From a large pool of audiotaped sessions conducted by 15 therapists, 60 instances of such discrete hearty laughter were examined to discover how these events were brought about (Gervaize, Mahrer, & Markow, 1985). Five therapist operating procedures were identified as leading to the laughter and available for therapists who value this particular in-session event.

Here are two ways of integrating operating procedures into your own way of doing therapy. Each of these ways calls for the therapist to be open to studying tapes and transcripts, especially of other therapists, and to studying the findings of clinical researchers who follow this discovery-oriented line of research inquiry. The immediate consequence is that therapists will then have the opportunity of integrating new operating procedures into their own therapies, and the indirect consequence is that the integration of psychotherapies will occur at the level of concretely specific operating procedures.

Consequences for the Field of Psychotherapy

I am a proponent of this second strategy, and it is understandable that I am excited about the likely consequences on the field of psychotherapy of adopting this strategy:

There will be a public pool of concretely specific operating procedures. Quite independent of any theory of psychotherapy or of any particular therapeutic approach, there likely will be a public pool of the concretely specific operating procedures used by most therapies. I foresee a whole marketplace of these operating procedures, the working tools of the various therapies, perhaps organized into groups and packages.

What is more, these concretely specific operating procedures will be public. Each therapy will be acknowledged as a theory of psychotherapy, as a conceptual body of thought that is more than a mere collection of its own operating procedures. Each therapy may have its own favorite operating procedures; but the acknowledgement will be that the pool is indeed public so that other therapies can add to and select from it. No therapy will *own* any operating procedure, although each therapy will *use* its own special set.

The operating procedures of each therapy will undergo development and change. As we build a public pool of operating procedures, each therapy will be free to adopt new operating procedures and modify them to fit the therapy. In other words, the working technology of each therapy will undergo development and change. Psychodynamic therapies may well find useful a few of the operating procedures that bioenergetic therapies use, and client-centered therapy may adopt a few of the operating procedures added to the public pool by Gestalt therapies.

Some therapies have gotten stuck because they tend to rely on a few operating procedures that were born with the therapies and have always been *identified with* the therapies. This means that such therapies as psychoanalysis and client-centered therapies will be faced with the possibility of an exciting period of growth and development while their theories of psychotherapy may remain intact. On the other hand, therapies that have grown up with only a small set of operating procedures will be faced with the challenge of either going out of existence or adding new and effective operating procedures.

There will be increased integration among therapies at the level of concretely specific operating procedures. I foresee a measure of integration as therapies share operating procedures. But this will be only a *measure*, for several reasons. One is that the same operating procedure may be crucial and central to one therapy, while playing only an ancillary role in other therapies. A second reason is that I foresee only a few operating procedures being useful to many therapies, and most operating procedures being useful to only a few other therapies. A third reason is that therapies will tend to use the same operating procedure under distinctive therapeutic conditions. Some therapies may use a procedure only rarely and under specific conditions, while others will use that procedure more commonly and under more frequent and varying conditions. Yet the net consequence will be a measure of increased integration at the level of concretely specific operating procedures.

There will be some reduction in the overall number of psychotherapies. As we develop a public pool of operating procedures, and as there is acceptance of the distinction between theories of psychotherapy and operating procedures, the net consequence likely will be some reduction in the overall number of psychotherapies. There are some therapies whose major claim to distinction lies in certain operating procedures. Such therapies have little or no distinctive theories of psychotherapy, but rely on those few distinctive operating procedures. Such therapies are easily incorporated into other therapies that find those operating procedures useful. Many eclectic or integrative therapies combine many of these operating procedures into a single overall therapy. I foresee the gradual demise of those therapies that are essentially built around a few operating procedures, and the gradual trend will be toward a reduction in the overall number of psychotherapies. *There will be a renaissance of the thoughtful study of psychotherapy by psychotherapists.* As we gain increased appreciation of operating procedures, a number of ingredients will be added to the *research* study of psychotherapy. One is that researchers will concentrate even more on the operating procedures used, on the *conditions* under which they are used, and on the in-session and extra-session *consequences* of using these operations. This is already happening. It will enjoy much further study.

Secondly, I foresee the addition of psychotherapists to the ranks of psychotherapy researchers. Some psychotherapists will wear both hats. They will be practitioners, and they will also be researchers who use research designs, research instruments and therapeutic measures, statistics and samples. Other psychotherapists will extend the definition of research to include the thoughtful study of psychotherapy by psychotherapists. Long before researchers applied their technical wares to psychotherapy, thoughtful therapists studied the concrete operations that occurred in therapy. It is ironic that this tradition led to Carl Rogers and his colleagues pioneering in the use of research technology to study the actual operating procedures they found in psychotherapy and that, ever since, the use of research technology has crowded out the thoughtful study of psychotherapy by psychotherapists. Today there is a great deal of sophisticated research technology applied to psychotherapy, and the word "research" has come to exclude the thoughtful study of psychotherapy by psychotherapists. Thus I foresee the renaissance of the thoughtful study of psychotherapy by psychotherapists, especially in what may be termed "discovery-oriented" research.

Chapter 3

THE INTEGRATION OF THERAPEUTIC VOCABULARIES

There is a third strategy for integrating psychotherapies. Unlike the first, it does not include the development of substantive new theories of psychotherapy. Unlike the second strategy, there is no attempt to integrate the operating procedures used in the various therapies. Instead, the aim is to concentrate on the *vocabularies* of the various therapies, and to integrate the actual terms, phrases, and words that comprise therapeutic argots.

The purpose of this chapter is to describe two quite different meanings of this strategy; to propose a workable method for carrying out one of these two meanings; and to outline the consequences for the field of psychotherapy of pursuing each of the two meanings.

TWO MEANINGS OF INTEGRATING THERAPEUTIC VOCABULARIES

There are two meanings of trying to integrate therapeutic vocabularies. They differ not only in their meaning, in how to carry out the strategy of integrating therapeutic vocabularies, but also in their implications for the field of psychotherapy.

The big meaning: A single common integrative vocabulary

There are several considerations motivating those who work toward a single common integrative vocabulary. One is a conviction that a fair proportion of terms really have quite similar meanings even though they occur in different approaches. These integrationists believe that much of the difference between approaches lie in their vocabularies. Therapies tend to develop their own technical vocabularies which give the impression of more differences than really exist between therapies. Much of this apparent distinctiveness would wash away if we had a single common vocabulary.

Secondly, we could all communicate so much better with one another if we had a single common vocabulary instead of the many fragmented languages we have today. Some languages are so technical that they are quite effective deterrents to other therapists who may want to become familiar with those approaches. We almost need a dictionary so that a client-centered therapist can understand cognitive behavior therapy or a psychodynamic therapist communicate with a rational-emotive therapist.

Third, it would be so much better for communicating with the uninitiated if we had a single common language. Those outside the field of psychotherapy are easily put off by the many different vocabularies we use. Undergraduate and graduate students are easily confused by the lack of a single common psychotherapeutic vocabulary. The lay public is understandably unable to grasp our many technical vocabularies. How would professions such as economics or medicine communicate with the public without a more or less single common vocabulary?

Fourth, it would be good for the field of psychotherapy itself to have a reasonably scientific single vocabulary. Obviously this would be helpful to research. But it would also be important for clinical practice if we could adopt a single common language that is rigorous and systematic.

Armed with these considerations, it is easy to set out to develop a common vocabulary. What should this new vocabulary be like? What are the criteria of such a language which we might all adopt? There are answers offered by proponents of this big meaning of integrating therapeutic vocabularies (cf. Norcross,

1987). For one, it should be the language of scientific psychotherapy (Goldfried, 1980; Ryle, 1978; Sarason, 1979). It should not be too steeped in the theory of any one approach. Its words should be neutral rather than reflecting the jargon of one approach (Goldfried & Padawer, 1982; Murgatroyd & Apter, 1986). It should include terms that refer to the psychotherapeutic events we all deal with in our work. These are the proposed requirements offered by the behavior therapists who have been the most zealous proponents of the single common vocabulary. Accordingly, ". . . the language from cognitive psychology has been suggested as offering us a set of relatively neutral concepts, having a minimal theoretical superstructure, and being closely related to the kinds of phenomena that we all see in our clinical work" (Goldfried, 1982b, p. 34; see also Arnkoff, 1980; Merluzzi, Rudy, & Glass, 1981; Ryle, 1987; Trower & Turland, 1982; Turk & Speers, 1983).

In behavior therapy's efforts to have its vocabulary elevated to super-language, perhaps the landmark events have been the pioneering attempt to approximate psychoanalytic terms such as insight and repression by learning terms such as conditioning, inhibition, and differentiation (French, 1933), Dollard and Miller's (1950) monumental effort to blend psychoanalytic concepts into the language of learning theory, and the capitulation to the supremacy of a learning theory vocabulary by a dean of psychoanalysis, Franz Alexander (1963).

Behavior therapy leads the pack in offering its vocabulary as the mother tongue of psychotherapy. There are a few other candidates, but not many. Driscoll (1984, 1987), for example, suggests that we adopt plain, ordinary, everyday terms from ordinary, everyday language. I like the idea of replacing technical jargon with plain, everyday terms. But I would be hesitant to adopt the implicit theory of psychotherapy built into much of ordinary language (cf. Messer, 1987). Nevertheless, the language of behavior therapy is perhaps the leading contender. Yet the attempt to generate an overall common vocabulary is coupled with some serious problems. It is one thing to sketch out the advantages of having a single common vocabulary. However, that almost implies a process of high-level negotiation wherein representatives of the various vocabularies cooperatively develop a friendly common language system. What typically occurs is jarringly different. Proponents of one approach challenge other approaches by saying that our vocabulary shall be the supreme one. Our terms will replace yours. This is quite a different sort of proposition. Now the idea of a single common vocabulary begins to take on an ominous cast.

As might be expected, proponents of each therapeutic vocabulary are steadfast in upholding their own language, and in aggressively demonstrating that their own language is likewise capable of incorporating other languages. The psychoanalytic vocabulary is quite able to incorporate the concepts of other approaches (Silverman, 1974). Any concept in any approach is exceedingly vulnerable to description within other vocabularies. For example, the concept of systematic desensitization can be handled by vocabularies as widely dispersed as Freudian, cognitive, Sullivanian, and Jungian (Brown, 1967; Goldstein & Stein, 1976; Weitzman, 1967; Wilkins, 1971.)

Indeed, if the proponents of the various psychotherapies set themselves to show that their vocabulary can incorporate other vocabularies, my conviction is that each can be successful. The game would be little more than vocabulary-flexing in which each vocabulary swallows the others so that the final swallower ". . . is viewed as the 'primary' language, a sort of mother tongue that can wholly encompass the ideas and observations of the other . . ." (Schacht, 1984, p. 115).

For the winner, the prize would be the status of supreme mother tongue, thereby gaining a solid advantage over the inferior languages. The problem is not only that each language can incorporate the others, but also that so many terms in so many approaches are so exceedingly loose. This looseness makes it easy to incorporate these terms into some invading vocabulary. At the same time, however, this selfsame looseness allows the proponents of these terms to reject incorporation by the new vocabulary as not capturing the essence of the terms; they cannot be translated without doing harm to the real meaning. All in all, I agree with those who hold that the intent to develop a single common language is not only faced with insurmountable linguistic, semiotic, and communication problems, but also that what are typically proposed as neutral terms ". . . are not in any absolute sense neutral terms, *nor can they be*" (Messer, 1986, p. 385); that the whole venture is a grand example of the "myth of a common language" (Messer, 1986, p. 385); and that most proponents of most vocabularies have solid bases for resisting the whole venture (cf. Kazdin, 1984; Koch, 1964; Messer, 1986, Schacht, 1984). Nonetheless, the big meaning of integrating therapeutic vocabularies is that of trying to arrive at a single overarching common vocabulary. It is ambitious, complex, and fraught with problems.

The little meaning: Terms sharing the same psychotherapeutic referent event

The other meaning of integrating psychotherapeutic vocabularies is much simpler, much more limited, and far more pedestrian. It does not aim toward the establishing of a supreme mother language. It does not even deal with terms that are part of a theory of psychotherapy. That is, it has little or nothing to do with higher-order descriptions of patients, with therapeutic goals and directions of change, with principles of therapeutic change, nor with general therapeutic strategems. It does not refer to the concepts of any theory of psychotherapy. The little meaning starts out with a general disclaimer that terms belonging to a theory of psychotherapy are outside the scope of integration.

Once we exclude terms belonging to the theory of psychotherapy, there is no longer any way for there to be a single common language for all psychotherapies. This is a grand hope of the first meaning of this strategy, but it is beyond the intent of the little meaning of integrating vocabularies. In order to qualify as a common language, the vocabulary must include something about general therapeutic stratagems, principles of therapeutic change, therapeutic goals and directions of change, higher-order descriptions of patients. The big meaning of integrating therapeutic vocabularies will do this. The little meaning declines.

What, then, is included in the little meaning? It pertains to the actual, ongoing, immediate, working events of psychotherapy. It is based on the idea that some of these terms share the same referents, the same point-to-able events rather than to the theory of psychotherapy (cf. Goldfried, 1987). A term in one vocabulary refers to virtually the same events as a different term in another vocabulary. These terms may refer to how and what the therapist is being and doing, to how and what the patient is being and doing, and to their interaction or relationship. Right now, one perspective says that the therapist is interpreting, while another perspective uses the phrase "orienting the patient." One perspective says that right here the therapist and patient are engaging in a working alliance, yet another perspective uses the word "encounter." The patient is engaging in imagery, says one perspective, while another uses the term vicarious learning. Right here the patient is undergoing heightened experiencing, yet another perspective refers to this as affective arousal. Perhaps these terms refer to similar psychotherapeutic events.

The referential meaning has to do with something happening right here in the therapeutic process, to something the therapist or the patient is doing, to something we can observe on a videotape. The terms refer to events right here before us rather than to concepts or constructs that are parts of a theory of psychotherapy.

This is the little meaning of integrating therapeutic vocabularies. It is limited to terms that point to actual therapeutic events. Even so, it is further limited to perhaps a small proportion of these terms. This second meaning of integrating vocabularies holds hopes that are very down to earth. It is not going to make a radical change in the integration of psychotherapies. At best, it may show that some terms, from different approaches, have rather similar referential meanings. It will never arrive at a common language for all or most psychotherapies. It is not designed to do so.

It Is Fruitless to Develop a Common Integrative Therapeutic Vocabulary

Most of the terms in the field of psychotherapy refer to theories of psychotherapy. Indeed, these words are drenched in some theory or another. They refer to the useful material to be elicited, to how to listen and what to listen for, to higher-order ways of describing the patient and the target of change, to the therapeutic goals and the directions of change, to the principles of therapeutic change, and to general therapeutic stratagems (Figure 1). Because these are theoretical terms, arising out of and having meaning in terms of a given theory of psychotherapy, there can be no common vocabulary. The terms from one theory cannot be replaced by the terms from some other theory, nor can new terms be invented that have the same theoretical meaning across all or even most theories of psychotherapy. It is fruitless to try and develop a common theoretical vocabulary.

Many terms refer to deeper personality processes. Yet they too are theoretical, and cannot permit a common theoretical vocabulary. There are terms such as archetypes, deeper and basic potentials, unconscious wishes, primary process material, social drives, core personal constructs, irrational beliefs, and hundreds more. Each is steeped in its own parental theory, and therefore cannot be reduced to or replaced by either terms from some other theory or by terms which are held as universally applicable. No matter what component of a theory of psychotherapy we focus upon, the terms cannot accommodate a common vocabulary because of their theoretical meaning. The only way to have a common theoretical vocabulary is to have a common theory of psychotherapy—and that is not the way things are in this field.

Those who propose a set of criteria for a common language agree that the terms should not be steeped in theory. Instead, they say, the terms should be neutral. But no theoretical term can be neutral. No term can be part of a common language when it has meaning in any theory of psychotherapy. Once a term refers to any component of a theory of psychotherapy, it loses its chance to be a natural part of a common therapeutic vocabulary. Watch out for terms that appear to be neutral, for they either are so generalized that they have little or no meaning or they mask a particular theoretical approach. Those who propose terms from cognitive theory either explicitly or implicitly adhere to a cognitive theory of psychotherapy. For example, Ryle (1978, 1982, 1984, 1987) stoutly proposes a common cognitive vocabulary that is dressed in neutral terms for other approaches to accept. The ways that "neurotics" operate are described with terms that are indeed neutral: traps, dilemmas, and snags, as three representative words from a neutral mother tongue. Yet a closer inspection of the meaning of these words reveals the clear cognitive theoretical structure underlying each term. The term "traps" refers to neurotic negative cognitive assumptions about oneself that lead to behavior that provokes consequences confirming these negative cognitive assumptions. If you accept the apparently neutral words, you buy the theoretical structure of cognitive psychology. Terms may appear neutral enough, but their meanings are not likely to be regarded as neutral by proponents of other approaches. It will not work to package a vocabulary from one approach in apparently neutral terms and then try to sell the vocabulary to just about everyone.

What is left? Mainly there remains the power struggle among the various therapies to get their terms elevated to that of the common tongue. Should we all speak the language of experiential psychotherapy? What about the language of psychoanalysis or Jungian analysis? How about rational-emotive therapy's vocabulary? Whatever vocabulary seeks to get itself universally adopted will have to win the power struggle over all other vocabularies. The effort, though inviting, is, in my opinion, fruitless.

If it is fruitless to try and develop a common integrative therapeutic vocabulary, is there any way of effecting some degree of integration among the many therapeutic vocabularies? I believe there is.

A METHOD FOR INTEGRATING TERMS SHARING THE SAME REFERENTIAL MEANING

Not all psychotherapeutic terms are theoretical, i.e., have their predominant meaning within a body of theoretical constructs. Most do, but not all. It is with these other terms that we have an opportunity to integrate vocabularies.

Those who favor integrating terms into a common vocabulary say that some special terms refer to observable events in psychotherapy. Their meaning lies in these referential events, in things that occur in the *observables* of psychotherapy, rather than in *theory*. If we look at Figure 1, some terms refer predominantly to operating procedures, to what the therapist does, to concretely specific events outside of the theory of psychotherapy. We can add to this all the terms that refer to what the patient does, as along as all of this again refers to concretely specific, observable events in psychotherapy. If we say that the patient is crying or laughing or slapping the arm of the chair, these terms are not predominantly buried in some particular theory of psychotherapy. The key to generating an integrative vocabulary is that some terms refer to the events that are concretely and specifically observable in the ongoing events of psychotherapy, and outside of the theory of any psychotherapy. Here is where some work can be done.

But the work of integrating these terms is limited. There is no intent to develop a mother tongue. All we will accomplish is to say that these few terms share the same, or very similar, referential meanings in regard to the concretely observable events in the process of psychotherapy. As indicated in the beginning of this chapter, this aim is simple, restricted and is not intended to generate a common language—merely to identify the few terms that warrant understanding as referring to the same events.

The method of locating those terms involves the careful work of clinical research. But how do we see *which* terms share similar referential meanings, and invite integration? How do we carry out this third integrative strategy? Here is one recommended way of going about this clinical research.

I suggest that the clinical researcher start with a sample of actual tapes from therapists representing a variety of approaches. These are to be complemented with verbatim transcripts. I also suggest that judges be used who are also representative of various approaches. In my own research team I have approximately 12 judges, each of whom represents a somewhat different therapeutic approach, with the team as a whole reasonably representative of a number of approaches.

This breadth is helpful in the work of identifying terms that are especially friendly to particular approaches.

Consider that each judge has a category system for identifying and describing what the therapist is doing, another for what the patient is doing, and a third for what is occurring between them. Consider also that these category systems include the terms from many different therapeutic approaches, including experiential therapy, psychodynamic therapy, behavior therapy, psychoanalytic therapy, reality therapy, and so on. Look at the first therapist statement. What terms from what vocabularies do the judges use to identify and describe what the therapist is doing in the initial statement? Do the same for the initial patient statement, and for all subsequent therapist and patient statements.

If you have a good enough set of category systems that contain enough terms from enough vocabularies, if you have an adequate design and qualified judges, you should be able to identify which terms from what vocabularies share similar referential meanings. If you have a sufficient amount of the right kinds of data, you might have some indication that these terms, from different therapeutic vocabularies, seem to share similar referential meanings. However, a few considerations are in order before the researcher can conclude that these terms from different vocabularies genuinely share the same or similar referential meaning.

One consideration is that the researcher must be careful to insure that the terms actually refer to the same or similar events. It must be shown that the referent is the same shared words or behaviors by the patient or therapist, or the exact interactive relationship. It is common that clinical research uses as its unit of study the complete statement of the therapist or patient, and this is generally defined as everything said by that person, preceded and followed by the words of the other. However, this still leaves latitude for the referent of one term to be different from the referent of the other even though both point generally to the same complete statement.

A second consideration is that the terms must evidence regular and consistent coterminality. Otherwise, when a set of terms evidence a moderate coterminality, it may well indicate that the terms only go together under given therapeutic conditions but not others, or the findings may be taken as indicating interesting clusterings, or the terms are parts of a larger meaning, or one is the larger category while the other is a subcategory. In other words, moderate pairings do not warrant integration of those terms (cf. Mahrer, Nadler, Dessaulles, & Gervaize, 1987).

Aside from these two considerations, such clinical research would identify which terms, from various vocabularies, have conspicuously similar referential meanings and could be included in an integrative vocabulary. My impression is that such clinical research would provide a small yield of terms that share the same referential meanings. It would, however, identify the general similarities and differences in terms that may be thought to be somewhat similar, and interesting clusters of terms from various approaches that go together under some conditions. All of this would shed a little light on terms that really share the same referential meanings and therefore provide the basis for a limited kind of integration of therapeutic vocabularies.

CONSEQUENCES FOR THE FIELD OF PSYCHOTHERAPY

Suppose we pursued the third strategy of trying to integrate therapeutic vocabularies. What would be the consequences for the field of psychotherapy? I suggest that the consequences would vary depending on which meaning of this strategy is adopted, the little meaning or the big meaning.

The little meaning: Increased clarification in the referential meanings of a small number of terms

I believe that there would be some genuinely interesting findings from clinical research that studied the referential meanings of terms from various therapeutic vocabularies. The findings would be interesting, but I expect they will have little to do with the integration of therapeutic vocabularies.

Once we exclude all those terms that refer to theoretical components of psychotherapy, there is little left to study. Most of the words have heavy theoretical meanings, and it appears that these cannot be integrated. What is left is a small pool of words referring mainly to the ongoing events of the therapy process. If clinical research sought seriously to discover the terms from various approaches that regularly and consistently pointed to the same referential events, my impression is that the most we could expect is a little more clarity in the referential meanings of a small number of these terms.

It is understandable that there is virtually no research on this matter. Its payoff is so slight that perhaps the major consequence would for users of terms that refer to ongoing therapeutic events to be a little more careful in their use of these particular terms.

In general, the consequences of the little meaning of integrating therapeutic vocabularies would be slight. However, prospects for the big meaning would, I believe, be much more significant, and ominous.

The big meaning: Failure to achieve a common integrative vocabulary

Actual consequences of trying to achieve a common integrative vocabulary will likely be slight indeed because prospects for success are gloomy. While there will probably be sporadic efforts by individuals and professional committees to develop such a mother tongue, it seems that such efforts will be accompanied with all the hallmarks of failure in spite of the honest efforts of those spurred on by the vision. However, it is likely that the sheer attempts to develop such a common vocabulary and to have it generally accepted will provide its share of more ominous consequences for the field of psychotherapy.

The big meaning: Demonstrations of mutual vocabulary-swallowing

It is likely that a number of attempts will be made to elevate one vocabulary above others. Behavior therapists seem to be most prone to offer their vocabulary as the supreme vocabulary of psychotherapy. There are always frameworks that seek to cut across all approaches, and to provide a super-vocabulary from some communication approach or general systems schema. I foresee a certain amount of mutual vocabulary-swallowing in which threatening and threatened approaches must show that they can incorporate some other vocabularies.

The big meaning: Competitive struggles for the status of super-vocabulary

I foresee two kinds of competitive struggles among proponents of different vocabularies. One is the big struggle for having my vocabulary accepted as the established and acknowledged vocabulary of psychotherapy. That is serious, and will usually involve the major approaches. Behavioral therapies and psychoanalytic-psychodynamic approaches will be jostling and sparring with one another in this competitive struggle. The smaller competitions will be over key words and terms and phrases. Is the whole enterprise to be called psychotherapy, or will we move in the direction of psychotherapy and counseling and behavior therapy and casework and psychoanalysis and other special terms? Will terms such as neurotic, symptoms, psychopathology, ego, projection, and unconscious develop a neutral cast and become part of the common psychotherapeutic vocabulary? Or will such terms be recognized as belonging to the psychodynamic-psychoanalytic language? Whether we are looking at the possibility of a whole super-vocabulary or the destiny of particular words and phrases, the stakes are high, and the likely consequence for the field of psychotherapy is that of increased competitive strugglings, with little constructive payoff.

Chapter 4

THE INTEGRATIVE SUPER-FRAMEWORK

The purpose of this chapter is to describe and discuss a fourth strategy for integrating psychotherapies. In an important sense, this is the most ambitious of the strategies, for it is aimed at elevating a particular psychotherapeutic approach into that of the super-framework, the psychotherapy that integrates the various psychotherapies. It is the supreme super-framework.

Proponents of many psychotherapies privately believe that their approach is best and, in a truly fair and just world, should be the supreme super-framework. A variation on this private hope is the belief that other psychotherapies may be adequate for the lesser, more mundane jobs, but my approach is clearly the most effective, the deepest, the noblest, and the most appropriate for those who deserve the finest. Psychoanalysts occasionally believe that there are *psychotherapies,* and *then* there is *psychoanalysis,* the top rung of the ladder. I would love to indulge a secret dream that experiential psychotherapy will emerge as the crowning super-framework, except that I am convinced that experiential psychotherapy cannot integrate all or even most other psychotherapies; and I also believe that there can be no single super-framework because we have no single super-theory of human beings. So my secret hopes for experiential psychotherapy are, unfortunately, more limited. Yet this strategy is perhaps the most ambitious and promises the most powerful and sweeping implications for the field of psychotherapy. The first strategy merely involves the integrative development of substantive new theories of psychotherapy. There is *no* super-framework, no elevation of one approach over others. The second strategy merely invites each approach to use the public marketplace of operating procedures. Again, there is no place here for some super-framework. The third integrative strategy has high hopes of establishing a super-vocabulary across the various psychotherapies, yet the present fourth strategy goes much further. It seeks to establish more than merely a vocabulary as preeminent; it seeks to elevate a particular therapeutic framework as superior. All in all, this strategy calls for close examination because it is ambitious, and because it promises powerful implications for the field of psychotherapy.

RATIONALE FOR THE DEVELOPMENT OF AN INTEGRATIVE SUPER-FRAMEWORK

The development of an integrative super-framework rests on a number of principles or propositions which constitute the rationale and which also serve to identify the worthiness of a given candidate.

There is a need for an integrative conceptual system for students in the psychotherapy-related professions

The rationale goes like this. Students learn three or five or more different approaches to psychotherapy, each with its own theory of personality, theory of psychopathology, theory of psychotherapy, techniques and methods. Not only can all of this be confusing, and thereby slow down the student's development toward understanding the field of psychotherapy, but it also deprives the student of a solid foundation into which the various approaches can be placed. Students need an integrative framework. If this framework is there from the very beginning of their graduate training, it organizes and simplifies their learning of the various approaches. If the emphasis on an integrative framework occurs toward the end of their training, it provides a way of putting together the knowledge and experience they acquired during their academic and internship training. Accordingly, graduate training ". . . should provide a system of analysis or a framework by which a multiplicity of theories and methods could be organized into an integrated understanding" (Reisman, 1975, p. 191; see also Halgin, 1985). This theme was echoed throughout the special section on training integrative/eclectic therapists in the Journal of Integrative and Eclectic Psychotherapy (Norcross, Beutler, Clarkin, DiClemente, Halgin, Frances, Prochaska, Robertson, & Suedfield, 1986).

There are multiple advantages to the approach which is chosen to provide the overarching integrative framework for thousands of students in psychology, social work, psychiatry, counseling, human relations, education, and other psychotherapy-related fields. I would certainly nominate experiential psychotherapy, but I would expect stiff competition from client-centered therapy, psychoanalytic therapy, psychodynamic therapy, all the behavior therapies, as well as the therapies that explicitly present themselves as offering an integrative framework. These integrative and eclectic frameworks are more than a general system for putting together other therapies. They are systems of psychotherapy in and of their own right. This is why Robertson (Norcross et al., 1986, p. 91) can say, "I expect that before long, basic psychotherapy texts will include four (rather than three) theoretical orientations: psychodynamic, phenomenological/humanistic, behavioral/cognitive, and integrative/eclectic." So the rationale is not only that students need a system for integrating all the other therapeutic approaches, but also that there is a therapeutic approach which serves as a fine therapeutic approach while managing to integrate all others. Make way for the integrative super-framework.

Each psychotherapy gets at a piece of the larger truth, so if we combine the various pieces we get closer to the real truth

Experiential psychotherapy comes from an existential-humanistic theory which accepts a very particular position on some key issues in the philosophy of science (Mahrer, 1978a). In general, this philosophy of science holds that there are multiple ways of describing whatever is taken as reality (Feigl, 1953; Fiske, 1971; Kantor, 1953; Koch, 1981; Mahrer, 1962; Messer, 1986; Royce, 1982; Schacht, 1984). Any event is open to description by means of constructs and concepts from multiple approaches, multiple perspectives. An event may be described and understood by means of constructs from, for example, physics or economics or theology or anthropology or psychology. Within psychology, for example, any event may be described from the constructs of learning theory or existential-humanistic theory or psychoanalytic theory or any other psychological body of constructs. No body of constructs is accepted as more "basic" than any other. Each body of constructs is accepted as its own distinctive mode of describing and understanding the event, and no body of constructs is necessarily reducible to some more basic or fundamental body of constructs; there is no hierarchy of sciences, with the constructs of one body reducible to the constructs of the other.

In this philosophy of science, each body of constructs has its own conception and construction of truth, reality, the basic stuff. Nor is a better or more realistic or truthful conception of truth or reality or basic stuff obtained by combining, adding, or integrating constructs from several bodies of constructs or theories.

With regard to theories of psychotherapy, this philosophy of science holds that each distinctive theory of psychology may have its own way of listening to and observing the events, i.e., to what the patient may be described as saying or doing or behaving or meaning. There is no real truth, or something the patient is *really* doing or saying or behaving or meaning above and beyond what that theory *construes* by means of its own way of listening and observing. It also means that there is no larger or deeper or underlying truth or reality which can be arrived at by combining or integrating what each theory holds as its truth or reality. This philosophy of science invites each theory of psychotherapy to grow and develop to its fullest without being reduced to or combined with any other theory of psychotherapy.

There are many positions on these issues of the philosophy of science, on the assumed number of basic events, on the method of inquiry into these basic events, and on their assumed nature. Experiential psychotherapy and its parent existential-humanistic theory of human beings holds to one position on these issues. Other theories of psychotherapy, and their own parent theories of human beings, hold to other positions on these issues. A popular position is held by most proponents of integrative super-frameworks, whether their theory of psychotherapy is behavioral, psychoanalytic-psychodynamic, eclectic, or whatever. These proponents accept, explicitly or implicitly, a position in which it is assumed that there is a single basic reality, a single basic truth, and that each theory of psychotherapy may get at only one *piece* of this single truth or reality. Accordingly, it follows that if these several pieces are combined with one another, we get closer to the *real* truth, the real reality. If we can integrate the best of the various theories of psychotherapy, the consequent super-framework is better than the component theories. All of this makes sense only if you accept their position on the relevant issues in the philosophy of science.

Experiential psychotherapy holds to one position on these issues. Those who seek an integrative super-framework hold to a quite different position. There is at least one more position on these issues which is different from that held by the experiential theory of psychotherapy, but like ours and unlike that held by the integrative super-framework proponents, does not allow the pursuit of an integrative super-framework. This is the position which holds that there is only one basic reality or truth, and all other constructs or all other theories are fully reducible to it. For example, this position can accept that basic events are biological in nature, and all psychological constructs can and will ultimately be reducible to those of biology—to neurological, physiological, and other biological events. Many behavioral theorists accept this position. So too do many psychoanalytic-psychodynamic theorists. Accordingly, these theorists reject the search for a super-framework, and are forced to believe by their philosophy of science that their own theory is ultimately best, and that all other theories will ultimately be reducible to its constructs. These theories cannot seek to combine or integrate pieces of several theories into a single larger whole. Rather, the work is to reduce the constructs of all other theories into their own, ultimately.

Those who seek to develop an integrative super-framework therefore tend to accept the idea that each psychotherapy may well get at a piece of the larger truth; so if these various pieces can somehow be combined, the result is a better theory of psychotherapy. Take the various principles of therapeutic change, for example. If some theories count upon experiencing as the way to therapeutic change, and if other theories count upon insight-understanding, and if each seems effective and "right," then a better theory is one which encompasses both experiencing and insight-understanding. If some theories of psychotherapy use "nonspecific" variables as effective ingredients of change, and if other theories use unique variables as effective ingredients, then it follows that a system is needed which encompasses both. "A theoretical system is needed that is sufficiently broad to encompass both the nonspecific and unique variables inherent in numerous theories. . ." (Beutler, 1983, p. 2). This is a sensible position for those who seek a super-framework. It is much less sensible for those who accept the other positions in the philosophy of science cited above.

I suggest that those who hold to the proper philosophy of science that allows for a super-framework should continue the work of integrating pieces from other theories which share the same philosophy of science and the same hope of a super-framework. The work can continue with like-minded theories of psychotherapy. But the development of a super-framework cannot occur with theories such as experiential theory. It holds to a different philosophy of science, and its philosophy of science has no place for super-frameworks. Here is a real clash. The super-framework philosophy of science believes that all theories of psychotherapy can contribute to the super-framework. In contrast, the philosophy of science of experiential theory and its sister theories says no, it cannot be done, do not try to assimilate me. Perhaps a reasonable compromise is to pursue the development of a super-framework only within those theories with friendly philosophies of science.

A theory really should have a friendly philosophy of science because the development of a super-framework generally means the end of the theory. Whatever framework elevates itself as super-framework is predominant, and the approaches that are included within the super-framework are diminished into fragmentary and incomplete components. Therapists who cling to these theories are guilty of being inferior, limited, fragmentary, incomplete: "Of course, an implication of global encompassing resolutions is that therapists who subscribe to particular theories are operating with only fragmentary understanding and imposing unnecessary restrictions on their practice" (Stiles, Shapiro, & Elliott, 1986, p. 174).

The work of developing an integrative super-framework rests on a philosophy of science in which it is assumed that each psychotherapy gets at a piece of the larger truth, so if we combine the various pieces we get closer to the real truth. But this is only a second part of the rationale for developing a super-framework. There is more.

An integrative super-framework can best fit the canons of science

Any theory of psychotherapy should strive to be scientific. Any theory which seeks the status of super-framework should therefore demonstrate that it best fits the canons of science. Such thinking turns attention to what the canons of science are taken to be, and which theories then best fit them. Here are some canons of science accepted by some of the theories which also qualify as meeting these canons:

(a) A scientific theory of psychotherapy exemplifies "the laws of human behavior." Just what are these laws? As articulated by proponents of behavior therapies, these laws of human behavior include, for example, the laws of effect, reinforcement, punishment, and extinction (Forsyth & Strong, 1986; Frankel, 1984). If these really are the laws of human behavior, then, sadly, the experiential theory of psychotherapy is not scientific, fails to meet the canons of science, and must withdraw from contention as a super-framework. Unfortunately, experiential theory would be joined by psychoanalytic theory, client-centered theory, Jungian analysis, Gestalt theory, and legion other theories. Who would remain? It looks as if only the behavioral theories of psychotherapy would be left to exemplify "the laws of human behavior," to meet the canons of science.

It seems to me that the framing of whatever are taken to be the laws of human behavior is part of the domain of *theories of human beings* rather than theories of psychotherapy. Every theory of human beings faces the issue of spelling out its propositions and assumptions about human beings and their behaviors. Accordingly, the issue becomes one of *which* theory of human beings accepts what *laws* of human beings. There well might be different "laws of human behavior" articulated by a biosocial theory of human beings, a psychoanalytic theory of human beings, an existential-humanistic theory of human beings, and a social learning theory of human beings. I am not impressed that some introductory psychology texts might pronounce "the scientific laws of human behavior" as including the laws of effect, reinforcement, punishment, and extinction. Each theory of human beings can dress up its own catechism of dogmatic laws of human behavior, and whichever theory is regnant will teach its own laws as basic, incontrovertible, and even scientific. Be wary of super-framework candidates who proclaim that they represent the scientific laws of human behavior.

(b) A scientific theory of psychotherapy rests on a solid foundation of knowledge in fields such as psychology, anthropology, biology, sociology, chemistry, and so on. According to this second canon, a framework that spans more of the basic human, social, and behavioral sciences is best fitted as a super-framework. Accordingly, the super-framework ". . . involves all levels of the human organism: biological, psychological, social, cultural, environmental" (Norcross et al., 1986, p. 91).

While I can accept this as a canon of one approach to the philosophy of science, I cannot accept this as a canon of all science. In the philosophy of science accepted by the existential-humanistic theory of human beings (Mahrer, 1978a), each body of scientific constructs may yield a full description and understanding of its events, and, symmetrically, equally full descriptions and understandings may be provided by psychology, anthropology, biology, sociology, chemistry, and other bodies of constructs. The psychological description and understanding of an event is not increased by describing and understanding that event from the perspective of anthropology, biology, sociology, chemistry, and so on. For example, a patient who begins laughing at this point in the therapeutic session may be described and understood by means of an experiential theory of psychotherapy. A full and complete description and understanding of that laughter may be offered by the experiential theory of psychotherapy. While we may obtain more description and understanding of that patient's laughing from an anthropological description, from a biological and sociological and a chemical description, none of these adds to the *experiential* description of the laughter.

However, another philosophy of science does indeed accept that we know more about an event by combining descriptions from multiple scientific perspectives, and, therefore, a better and fuller description of the laughter is provided by the additional modes of understanding and description. If you accept this particular philosophy of science, then you will accept the canon that a framework which spans more of the basic human, social, and behavioral sciences is best fitted as super-framework. However, the experiential theory of psychotherapy joins with other theories to decline this particular canon as outside its own philosophy of science.

(c) A third canon of science is that a theory's concepts and constructs are to be operationally defined, and its treatment procedures are to be replicable (Frankel, 1984). I believe that most theories of psychotherapy would accept this canon. Indeed, this is quite similar to our seventh component of a theory of psychotherapy (Figure 1), namely that a theory is to define the specific operations, the conditions under which these operations are to be used, and the consequences of using those operations. However, it in no way necessarily follows that the theory of psychotherapy which best meets this canon is a super-framework. Demonstrating that a theory fulfills this canon is no evidence for adopting the theory as a super-framework.

(d) A fourth canon of science requires that a theory of psychotherapy is to rest on a solid foundation of research. However, the game-playing strategy here is to present your research as the best scientific research, and to identify the findings of your research as the cumulative body of scientific knowledge. Behavior therapists are eager to identify their research as the most scientific, and to accept their own research findings as the cumulative body of scientific knowledge (cf. Messer, 1986). While I fully accept the importance of careful research, I cannot accept the research models and designs of behavior therapy as the best for experiential psychotherapy and for other theories of psychotherapy which simply do not accept the behavioral model and designs. For example, I much prefer the approach to scientific research which accepts the in-therapy change paradigm rather than the extra-therapy outcome paradigm (Mahrer, 1985). Accordingly, I accept as the "solid foundation of research" those studies adhering to the former paradigm, while most behavior therapists would accept as the "solid foundation of research" those studies which adhere to the latter paradigm.

It is easy to agree that a theory of psychotherapy is to rest on a solid foundation of research. It is much more difficult to determine whose research is more scientific, what findings from what studies are to be regarded as the cumulative body of scientific knowledge, and which research models, designs, and paradigms are to be accepted as the more scientific. What is more, there is no necessary correspondence between the extent to which a theory of psychotherapy rests on a solid foundation of research and the theory thereby qualifying as a super-framework. A theory can gain the prize as resting on the most solid foundation of research while neither trying for nor qualifying as a super-framework.

Which theory of psychotherapy best fits the so-called canons of science? One reading sees behavior therapy as the best qualified because it ". . . is the most scientific approach to behavior change in the current psychological marketplace" (Frankel, 1984, p. 129). I neither accept behavior therapy as necessarily the most "scientific," nor would I accept behavior therapists' proposed canons of science, or the conclusion that the most "scientific" theory is thereby the best candidate for super-framework. Yet all of this remains a solid plank in the platform for the development of an integrative super-framework.

A comprehensive framework is needed to integrate the various areas of human functioning

This part of the rationale starts by asserting that there are various areas of human functioning, claiming that extant theories are limited in their coverage of these various areas, and then concluding that a framework is needed which comprehensively integrates these various areas of human functioning (cf. Birk & Brinkley-Birk, 1974).

Just what are the various areas of human functioning? There is almost no limit to the ways in which one can divide human functioning into areas. For example, we may recognize such areas as the recreational, sexual, vocational, aggressive, ideational, health, familial, cultural, political, spiritual, emotional, biological, social, and on and on. However, my impression is that most attempts to integrate other approaches into a super-framework identify each major approach as dealing with some given area of human functioning so that an integrative super-framework can include all these areas. Accordingly, the question would be that of identifying what area(s) of human functioning are generally handled by psychoanalytic/psychodynamic approaches, what others are handled by humanistic/experiential approaches, and which are handled by behavioral approaches.

In pursuing this line of reasoning, Prochaska and DiClemente (1982) divide areas of human functioning into the inner (psychic, subjective) and the outer (objective, environmental), and thereby conclude that an integrative approach combines both inner and outer: "An integrative approach sees a combination of the two approaches as providing a more balanced view that moves along the continuous dimensions of inner to outer control, subjective to objective functioning, and self- to environmentally-induced changes" (p. 281). In a modified reading, Goldfried (1982b) holds that there are three areas of human functioning, so that genuinely comprehensive approaches ". . . take into account the interplay between emotional, cognitive, and behavioral change. It is our contention that each of the three major approaches to therapy—psychodynamic, behavioral, and humanistic—has something to offer the practicing therapist" (p. 22). Concurring on the threefold areas of functioning as the emotional, the cognitive and the behavioral, Ellis (1976) concludes that rational-emotive therapy covers all these, and thereby offers a truly comprehensive integration.

Is a comprehensive super-framework really needed to integrate the various areas of human functioning? This means that you must first identify your version of the various areas of human functioning, then demonstrate that the major approaches are each limited to their own few areas, and then show how your super-framework covers all bases. Experiential psychotherapy does not accept any part of the rationale. It does not accept the several versions of whatever are taken to be the various areas of human functioning. It does not accept that experiential psychotherapy deals with and is limited to the psychically subjective, or the emotional. It does not accept that some super-framework is needed to integrate the various areas of human functioning, however they are described. Finally, it does not accept that the candidates for super-framework are or can be any more comprehensive than any of the other broad-gauged approaches such as the behavior therapies or the psychoanalytic-psychodynamic therapies (cf. Messer, 1986). I cannot accept that some comprehensive framework is needed to integrate the various approaches to human functioning. Yet this remains an important plank in the rationale.

Here are four planks in the rationale for the development of an integrative super-framework. Not all theories of psychotherapy would accept this rationale. As a proponent of experiential psychotherapy, I can appreciate this rationale and applaud its efforts and aims; but it falls outside the scope of an experiential psychotherapy, the theory of human beings, and the underlying philosophy of science upon which the theory rests. I do not accept the rationale used to justify a super-framework.

Nevertheless, many *do* accept the rationale, and there *are* super-frameworks.

SOME CONTENDERS FOR SUPER-FRAMEWORK

There are two classes of therapies that contend for the status of super-framework. One consists of therapies that are among the ranks, but which are motivated to present themselves as doing a good job of integrating many other therapies. Among these are cognitive therapy (Ryle, 1982, 1984), problem-solving therapies (Urban & Ford, 1971), rational-emotive therapy (Ellis, 1976, 1979), and Kelly's personal construct approach (Leitner, 1982). Such approaches to psychotherapy were typically not developed as super-frameworks, but their proponents claim that they do what a super-framework is supposed to do.

The second class includes systems that have been explicitly developed as eclectic frameworks to fulfill the job requirements of super-framework. Representative of the guiding principles of the movement is the trans-theoretical therapy of Prochaska and DiClemente (1982): "Developing within the zeitgeist of a search for a synthesis, transtheoretical therapy is moving toward a more comprehensive model of change. Transtheoretical therapy emerged from a comparative analysis of 18 leading therapy systems" (p. 277; see also Prochaska, 1979; Prochaska & DiClemente, 1984). Each of the eclectic frameworks aims at building upon the common features of a number of other therapies, generally a large number, and to integrate them into a single overall super-framework.

Although there have been many attempts to construct such eclectic super-frameworks, I regard the pioneering formal system to be that proposed by Thorne in 1967 and updated in 1980. In the current climate there are many fresh proposals of comprehensive super-frameworks that synthesize the common features of many other psychotherapies. Among the more prominent are those by Beutler (1983, 1986), Fuhriman, Paul, and Burlingame (1986), Garfield (1980, 1986), Hart (1983),

Lazarus (1976, 1981, 1985), Orlinsky and Howard (1987), and Palmer (1980).

CONSEQUENCES FOR THE FIELD OF PSYCHOTHERAPY

I foresee four consequences for the field of psychotherapy as enthusiasm for an integrative super-framework continues to flourish:

It is likely that the number of psychotherapies will continue to increase. After all, anyone is free to develop yet another psychotherapy which aims at organizing other therapies. Already the time has come when reviewers discuss the dozen or so different comprehensive frameworks (Dryden, 1986), and it is ominously foreboding of an ebullience of therapy proliferation when Dryden finds ". . . little evidence at present that the contributors . . . are drawing upon one another's work to a significant degree. This surprises and troubles me" (p. 374). The likelihood of increasing proliferation among those who follow this strategy also was hinted at by Garfield and Kurz (1977), observed by Messer (1986), and succinctly foretold by Goldfried and Safran (1986): "If this trend is carried to its extreme, we may ultimately end up with as many eclectic models as we currently have schools of psychotherapy. . ." (p. 464). I expect we will be presented with many more eclectic and integrative super-frameworks before the other consequences unfold.

The likely emergence of one or two predominant super-frameworks. For those who are bothered by so many different kinds of therapy, this strategy also offers the greatest hope, for the direction is toward perhaps one or two dominant super-frameworks. The rationale is not content with seven to twelve or so different super-frameworks. There should be only *one*, and it is likely that those who are genuinely enthusiastic about the development of a super-framework will spell out procedural rules whereby more or less objective means will reorganize the contenders into a genuine super-framework. The strategy can encompass both possibilities: many new therapies or a few predominant ones.

The winning super-framework will face the problems and delights of winning, and the component psychotherapies will face the future of losers. Whichever super-framework manages to become king of the therapeutic mountain will face inevitable challenges from developing new super-frameworks and also from alien other therapies such as psychoanalysis which, while perhaps not claiming to be a super-framework, nevertheless enjoys its reign as the supreme psychotherapy. The struggle for super-framework can easily call upon the energies of proponents in the academic, professional, political, administrative, and research domains. What is more, the component therapies that are incorporated into the super-frameworks will be relegated to the status of second-class citizenship, as inferior, less adequate, less inclusive, more incomplete, more fragmented. While struggles among competitive psychotherapies seem to be inevitable, the rationale underlying the development of super-frameworks adds a dimension of relentless seriousness to the field of comparative psychotherapies.

For better or for worse, the direction will be toward a monolithic, single philosophical and conceptual foundation for the field of psychotherapy. With the adoption of a super-framework comes enforced acceptance of a particular position on some basic issues in the philosophy of science, the acceptance of a particular set of presumed laws of human behavior, the elevation of a particular approach to research inquiry, the establishment of a given body of scientific knowledge, the adoption of a given schema for organizing the areas of human functioning, and the use of a single overall framework as an integrative foundation for all other psychotherapies. This establishment of a monolithic single truth foundation for psychotherapy is especially sardonic in light of the mission of both the International Academy of Eclectic Psychotherapists and its *Journal of Integrative and Eclectic Psychotherapy's* avowal to oppose the "one truth" barrier that they find so repugnant in the field of psychotherapy (Norcross, 1986b). For better or for worse, the field would be moved toward the "one truth" uniformity. To me, it would be for worse.

Chapter 5

INTEGRATING COMMONALITIES ACROSS APPROACHES

A fifth strategy starts with the idea that some therapies share common elements, that there are commonalities across some of many therapies. Accordingly, it makes sense that these therapies can integrate with one another along these shared nexus points of commonality. In this strategy, there is no explicit attempt to develop a super-framework, to integrate at the level of either their respective vocabularies or at the level of concretely specific working operations, nor to develop a substantive new theory of psychotherapy. It is its own distinctive strategy and meaning of integration.

THE RATIONALE FOR INTEGRATION IS THAT THERE ARE COMMONALITIES ACROSS PSYCHOTHERAPIES

The rationale holds that there are commonalities across psychotherapies, and therefore these psychotherapies can be integrated along the lines of their commonalities. But what are the propositions upon which this rationale rests? How and where do we set about looking for these commonalities? Even if we identify some commonalities, how does that justify integrating the respective therapies?

Do not try to uncover commonalities at the level of their parent theories of human beings. Most proponents of this strategy agree that it is rather fruitless to try to identify commonalities at the level of the parent theories of human beings. "In the search for commonalities, it is unlikely that we can ever hope to reach common ground at either the theoretical or the philosophical level" (Goldfried, 1980, p. 994). The tacit understanding is that, for example, an existential-humanistic theory and a psychobiological theory and a psychoanalytic theory of human beings would have quite different positions on such issues as the assumed number of basic events and their content, the origins of infants, the basic stuff of personality, the structure and model of personality, the construction of social realities, and similar matters at the theoretical and philosophical level. Those who are concerned with this strategy of integration may, however, identify rough similarities in these theories of human beings as broad-gauged intellectual movements. Thus, for example, the behavioral and the existential-humanistic intellectual movements may be seen as sharing a desire to work toward a better world, and to appreciate the human individual (Krasner, 1978). But as substantive theories of human beings, the acknowledged stance is that it is fruitless to try and uncover integrative commonalities at the level of the parent theories of human beings.

Do not try to uncover commonalities at the level of concretely specific operating procedures. Nor does it seem profitable to try to uncover commonalities at the level of concretely specific operating procedures. About all that one can conclude from this exercise is that *some* theories of psychotherapy share *some* operating procedures. Such a conclusion leaves little or no room for integrating the various psychotherapies. Demonstrated commonalities at this level offer little or no purchase value for doing much more than affirming that some therapies do indeed use similar working therapeutic operations.

Consider a few examples of commonality at this working level. It can be shown that psychodynamic-psychoanalytic therapists use such working operations as suggestion, reinforcement, approval and disapproval, operations that are ordinarily associated with other approaches (Dewald, 1971; see also Grinker, 1976). It has also been shown that client-centered therapists use some interpretations, a working operation generally identified with psychoanalytic-psychodynamic therapies (e.g. Mahrer, Nifakis, Abhukara, & Sterner, 1984; Mahrer, Sterner, Lawson, & Dessaulles, 1986). Not only do these kinds of findings offer little or no basis for integrating therapies, but they give a distorted picture of the nature and extent of commonality. While psychodynamic-psychoanalytic therapists may be shown to use reinforcement, it plays a minor role compared to the central role it assumes in the behavior therapies. Similarly, client-centered therapies may occasionally use interpretation, but it is anything but the backbone operation it is in psychodynamic-psychoanalytic therapies. Also, reinforcement and interpretation are used under quite different conditions and for quite different purposes in client-centered, behavioral, and psychodynamic-psychoanalytic therapies.

All in all, it is essentially unprofitable and somewhat misleading to pursue integration by uncovering commonalities at the level of concretely specific working therapeutic operations. The most promising zone is the theory of psychotherapy that stands between the parent theory of personality at one extreme, and the concretely specific operating procedures at the other (Figure 1). "It is at the level of abstraction between these two extremes where there exists the most promising potential in the search for commonality" (Goldfried, 1982b, p. 14).

Assert that there are commonalities in therapeutic goals and directions of change. If several theories of psychotherapy can be shown to share common goals and directions of change, then the rationale holds that these therapies may be integrated with one another. It seems reasonable to integrate therapies that try to accomplish the same thing. Yet it is not so easy to demonstrate that a number of therapies do indeed share common goals and directions of change.

For one consideration, a great deal depends upon the level of concreteness or generality. A conceptual analysis of a broad and representative sample of psychotherapies concluded that the appearance of commonality at high levels of generality easily gave way to significant differences as you looked more closely at the actual working goals and directions of change (Mahrer, 1967). This means that proponents of this integrative strategy are drawn toward rather high levels of generalization in order to assert that various therapies may be said to share common goals and directions of change. For example, in order to conclude that behavior therapy, transactional analysis, Gestalt, and ego analytic therapies share a set of common goals, Frankel (1984) must describe these therapies as agreeing that their patients are ". . . to directly act on their environments to change the things they can" and /or ". . . to come to peace with themselves, and to accept the things they cannot change" (p. 130). This is a high level of generalization in order to be able to show that these therapies have common goals.

A popular attempt to assert common therapeutic goals holds that essentially all psychotherapies aim at helping patients with their problems. As self-evident as this may appear, it too tends to wash away on closer scrutiny (Mahrer, 1985). Therapies differ exceedingly when problems are understood more carefully as including everything from problems as defined by referral sources to problems as voiced by complainants such as spouse, coworkers, or neighbors. There are the problems voiced by the patient spontaneously before or at the beginning of therapy, problems as they evolve and alter in the course of therapy, problems identified by psychological checklists and inventories, and problems conjointly defined by patient and therapist who try to figure out just what the problem is. Then of course there are problems from the perspective of the therapist who is outfitted with an inventive array of technical concepts and jargon with which to define and describe the problem. A group of therapists might well nod agreement with the idea that therapy helps patients with their problems, but each therapist would then set about articulating the problem in a distinctive way, and these difficulties multiply when you then face the issue of assessing whether or not therapy has helped the patient with the problem. The more carefully you look at the working and the evolving meaning of "the problem," the more the exercise sinks further and further into confusion.

Nevertheless, the rationale holds that various therapies have to be seen as sharing a measure of common therapeutic goals and directions of change. It would perhaps be nice if therapies indeed shared common therapeutic goals and directions of change. It is an appealing idea. But I am convinced that in practice most therapies set about richly different goals and directions of change. Regardless, the rationale requires that we accept the idea that therapies have a measure of commonality in their goals and directions of change, and therefore it makes sense to integrate therapies that share common goals and directions of change.

Assert that there are commonalities in principles of therapeutic change, and in general therapeutic stratagems. The rationale must be able to assert that there are commonalities across psychotherapies. If we do not look for commonalities at the level of the theories of human beings (Figure 1), nor at the other level of the concretely specific working therapeutic operations, where can we look for commonalities? If you look at Figure 1, it seems difficult to try and identify a fair number of therapies that elicit the same kind of therapeutic material; therapies can too easily be seen as differing here. It also seems difficult to say that many therapies listen and observe in the same way and make the same kind of sense of the data. If we move on to "higher-order description of patient and target of change," it again appears hard to say that many therapies are similar here. The section immediately above discussed the feasibility of trying to assert that various therapies share common therapeutic goals and directions of change, and concluded that this too is difficult to maintain.

That seems to leave us with principles of therapeutic change and with general therapeutic stratagems. It is my impression that the outlook is much more promising here, and that one can make a case that there are commonalities in these two components. In support of this contention, Strupp (1979) suggests that behavior therapists and psychodynamic therapists may employ different terminologies, but that there is a good measure of commonality in their principles of therapeutic change and also in the general therapeutic stratagems used to effect these principles of therapeutic change. Goldfried (1980) is even more direct in naming these as the two richest areas in the search for commonalities:

> . . . the possibility of finding meaningful consensus exists
> at a level of abstraction somewhere between theory and

technique which, for want of a better term, we might call *clinical strategies.* Were these strategies to have a clear empirical foundation, it might be more appropriate to call them *principles* of change. (p. 994)

The rationale for integrating therapies along the lines of their commonalities is served well by asserting that there are commonalities in these two areas or components of theories of psychotherapy: principles of therapeutic change and general therapeutic stratagems. Whether or not such commonalities have been demonstrated, and just what kinds of commonalities have been found are issues that go beyond the rationale. If you are a proponent of this fifth strategy, the rationale merely guides you into looking for commonalities in the principles of therapeutic change and also in the general therapeutic stratagems that are used by various therapies.

Assert that most therapies are rather similar in terms of effectiveness. The rationale holds that if various therapies are rather similar in their degree of effectiveness in getting the job done, then these therapies ought to have some commonalities, and therefore they may be integrated along the lines of their commonalities. There is a good measure of face sensibility in the rationale. After all, the rationale can be opened wider or narrower to accommodate different framings. At the wider range, if most therapies have the same general level of effectiveness, then there should be some features that are probably held in common, and these therapies can be integrated along these common features. At the narrower level, if a few therapies are more or less equally effective in working with a particular kind of patient or problem, and achieving a particular result, then again, those specialized therapies probably share some commonalities and there is room for integration along the lines of these commonalities.

This rationale is understandably unwelcome to many proponents of particular therapeutic schools, for they are prone to believe that their therapy is the most effective for whatever their therapy is supposed to accomplish. These proponents are not easily convinced that many therapies are equally effective in accomplishing the job. Accordingly, the rationale is wise to turn to research for its supporting evidence. What is more, reviews of research tend to lean in the direction of providing the needed support. In one summary of the outcome effects of many therapies, Smith and Glass (1977, p. 760) draw the friendly conclusion that " . . . the results of research demonstrate negligible differences in the effects produced by different therapy types" (cf. Smith, Glass, & Miller, 1980). Another review of research confirms that the outcome is much the same regardless of what the therapist does: "The paradoxical findings of outcome equivalence and content non-equivalence present a serious dilemma because they seem to imply that no matter what a therapist does, the end result is the same" (Stiles, Shapiro, & Elliott, 1986, p. 167). Even for those who cling to the distinctive effectiveness of their particular techniques, reviews of research are dispassionately unfriendly, for the research seems to indicate that these methods and techniques are indeed generally effective across all sorts of therapies: "reviews of outcome studies have concluded that there is little support for the differential effectiveness of techniques" (Halgin, 1985, p. 559). Alas, the research polls bring bad tidings for those who want to believe that their therapy is uniquely effective, and good tidings for those who are looking for commonalities.

If there is a fair measure of agreement that therapies are rather similar in terms of effectiveness, then we can begin looking for what these therapies share in common. As long as no one therapy is clearly superior in effectiveness, it makes sense to look for ways in which therapies have something in common; ". . . it is fair to state that no set of techniques or general approach has an agreed-upon basis for flaunting its superiority. Ambiguity on the superiority of any particular approach certainly has provided the climate for integrationism" (Kazdin, 1984, p. 143). As long as no approach is clearly superior, as long as so many therapies can claim equal effectiveness, integrationists can point proudly to the likely presence of commonalities. Nor does it matter whether therapies are effective or ineffective. It is their *similarity* that allows us to look for their common points.

Accept the proposition that if therapies share commonalities it follows that integration is warranted.   Let us consider the extreme case. Suppose that a number of therapies share all seven of the components of theories of psychotherapy (Figure 1), and that these therapies also are quite similar in terms of their effectiveness. It would seem most sensible that these therapies may be integrated with one another. However, I am aware of no instances where therapies are so very similar that they practically invite integration. Extreme cases are extremely rare. What does happen, however, is that some therapies do overlap where the earlier discussion says it is likely to occur, namely in regard to principles of therapeutic change and in general therapeutic stratagems.

Let us then turn to those instances in which some therapies do indeed share these two kinds of commonalities. If some therapies share common principles of therapeutic change and/or common therapeutic stratagems, does it follow that these therapies warrant integration along these lines? The rationale says yes. Indeed, the rationale hinges on this proposition. Let us take a closer look at this proposition.

In an analysis of what he terms the "fallacy of common elements," Schacht (1984) argues that identifying common elements in a number of psychotherapies does not warrant integrating these therapies:

> The justification for this search involves a belief that finding such common elements constitutes evidence that bears positively on the question of integration. . . . There is thus a tacit cumulative assumption to the search for common elements—as if each common element possessed a "quantum of integration," with the current total of such quanta reflecting the aggregate prospects for integration of the therapies. Despite frequent use of common elements as evidence for integration, there are no compelling reasons to accept such arguments. (p. 120)

I am inclined to agree with Schacht. Suppose that we focus on a particular principle of therapeutic change, e.g., the providing of a corrective emotional experience, and suppose that the claim is that this principle may be found in psychodynamic, client-centered, behavioral, and experiential therapies. According to the justifying rationale, just what is to be integrated among these four therapies? Do we integrate some of the concretely specific working operations for bringing about the corrective emotional experience? This would mean integrating such operating procedures as the patient's actually touching the snake without having a panic response, the use of empathic reflections within an atmosphere of unconditional positive regard, a well-timed interpretation about the transference neurosis, and the patient's being the deeper potential within the context of significant events prior to conception. If the therapists were inclined to borrow such a peculiarly mixed bag of operating procedures, they could easily do so under the second strategy, without having to show that all four therapies share a principle of change involving a corrective emotional experience. If they were disinclined to use this bag of operating procedures, I doubt if claiming that the four therapies all provide a corrective emotional experience would convince any of the therapists to start integrating all of the operating procedures. I am not persuaded that the claiming of shared principles of therapeutic changes, or shared general therapeutic stratagems, or any other shared commonalities, necessarily warrants the integration of these therapies. If integration refers to operating procedures, therapies can borrow these freely without justifying the act as integration.

If we do not "integrate" operating procedures, then just what do we integrate when several therapies are shown to accept the same principle of therapeutic change or general therapeutic stratagem? Do we integrate the other components? The soft implication is that this is not the only commonality. That is, if two therapies share the same principle of therapeutic change, then the two therapies should likewise share common goals and directions of change, higher-order description of the patient, general therapeutic stratagems, and so on. Yet these other common integratable components are seldom if ever demonstrated and seldom if ever demonstratable. Accordingly, the significance of common elements is highly questionable; ". . . the finding of common elements in behavioral and dynamic therapies is of uncertain significance unless these elements are also connected in a common system of functional relations or in a common structure of meaning" (Schacht, 1984, p. 121). In other words, the common element must be shown to have common connections with the other components of each theory of psychotherapy involved (Figure 1). Yet without such common connections to the other components of the theory, the assertion of a common element lacks a crucial basis for integrating the respective therapies.

All in all, the rationale for integrating therapies across commonalities seems to be on thin ground. It requires that we accept not only that therapies are rather similar in degree of effectiveness, not only that there indeed are commonalities in therapeutic goals and directions of change, in principles of therapeutic change, and in general therapeutic stratagems, but also that we accept the proposition that if therapies share commonalities it follows that integration is thereby warranted. The rationale is not very solid. I do not accept the rationale that therapies are to be integrated along the lines of their commonalities.

HOW TO DEMONSTRATE A GENUINE COMMONALITY

Indeed, I believe that the rationale is so thin that it is a fruitless venture to pursue a strategy of trying to integrate whatever is taken as common across some therapies. Even so, it seems somewhat unfair to foreclose the whole venture without taking a closer look (cf. Rosenzweig, 1936). After all, proponents are satisfied with the rationale, and have a lot of faith in this fifth strategy. For the believers, there should be ways to demonstrate that a genuine commonality exists. How can this be done?

Designate those theories of psychotherapy that share the commonality.   A proposed commonality will likely gain a fairer audience when the proponents designate those theories of psychotherapy that are involved. Once a proposed commonality is well described, it is rather unlikely that it is a shared denominator in all or even most therapies. It is better to limit the commonality to particular therapies than to act as if the commonality is just about universal.

Some propose a commonality that patients have an expectancy that therapy will be helpful, and that therapies rely upon and cultivate that expectancy (e.g., Frank, 1973; Marmor, 1976; Prochaska, 1979). Is this a common factor in all psychotherapies, in most, a few? While this is not specified, the strong implication is that it is a common factor across virtually every therapeutic approach. But too many therapies join experiential therapy in disclaiming this commonality. I suggest that it would be easier to demonstrate genuine commonalities if the proponents designate those therapies that accept them. Only *certain* therapies agree that patients coming to therapy have expectant readiness that therapy will help, and that therapists rely upon and cultivate this expectancy.

There really is no need for a commonality to be universal; yet many proponents of commonalities insist that they are. Indeed, I suggest that all you have to do is to designate those approaches that accept and manifest that commonality, and integration can proceed right along even if the commonality is not universal. Furthermore, it would be easier to proceed with integration if a commonality is *not* universal, but rather occurs within and across friendly therapies, regardless of how many; two are enough.

What would constitute acceptable evidence to conclude that the commonality does not fit a given psychotherapy? For example, experiential psychotherapy declines to describe patients as coming to therapy with an expectancy that therapy will be helpful, nor does experiential psychotherapy rely upon or cultivate that supposed expectancy. Instead, we hold that patients come to therapy on the basis of the same experiencings that account for their behavior in other parts of their lives. A patient may be geared toward psychotherapy as a means of being accepted and understood by the right kind of therapist-person. In therapy the patient may be able to massage her precious self. He may be able to gain in solace and nurturance. She may relate to the omniscient one, the grand savior, the strong parent, the one with whom she may be intimate and warm, a best friend, a kindly supporter who is on her side, the parental figure she never really had, the strong one to insure that she does not fall into a state of chaos, or any of a large number of role relationships. Experiential psychotherapy understands patients as turning to psychotherapy on the basis of these experiencings, played out within some kind of role relationship with a therapist. Our theory has little or no place for patients coming to therapy with an expectancy that therapy is helpful, especially in solving their preferred "problems." I suggest that theories be free to accept or decline the commonality, and that it is not necessary to prove that a commonality fits or does not fit.

It is simply too easy and too deceptive to describe a commonality as either fitting or not fitting some therapy. That is, it is easy to say that all patients who enter therapy can be described in terms of their experiencings at engaging in a role relationship with the therapist. In the same way, it is easy to say that all patients who enter therapy can be described as having an expectancy that therapy will be of help in their problems. Yet the two descriptions are quite different with regard to what the therapist actually does and how the therapist uses what the patient says and does in the beginning of therapy.

Whatever commonality is proposed, it is helpful to designate those therapies that accept it. It is not necessary to assert that all therapies manifest that commonality. Indeed, it is much too difficult to defend the commonality as extending across all or most therapies. All the strategy needs is to name whatever therapies do share the commonality.

Describe the commonality in terms that are reasonably concrete and specific rather than loose and general. It is difficult to spell out the commonality in terms that are reasonably concrete and specific, yet this is important for demonstrating a genuine commonality. If the commonality refers to a principle of therapeutic change or a therapeutic stratagem, use words that are sufficiently precise that one can justifiably say yes or no to its presence in a given therapy.

It is easy to frame commonalities at such a loose and general level that they are virtually tantamount to the definition of psychotherapy itself. Then all psychotherapies would be pulled to nod in agreement. For example, commonalities may be described as the conveying of a frame of reference and a value system, as offering a therapist-patient relationship, as providing support and release of tension (Marmor, 1976). Yes, most therapies would tend to agree that they do all that. And it is easy to conclude that these are commonalities. But such commonalities are not especially impressive, for they are far too loose and vaguely general. It takes more work to demonstrate that a proposed commonality really qualifies as a genuine commonality.

One popularly proposed commonality is that of the relationship between patient and therapist (e.g. Greenson, 1965, 1967; Luborsky, 1976; Strupp, 1979; Wilson & Evans, 1976, 1977). Indeed, the relationship is such a core feature of psychotherapy that it is almost a necessary part of the very definition of psychotherapy itself. But even as a principle of therapeutic change, "the relationship" deserves to be made substantially more specific and concrete before it qualifies as a genuine commonality. If we do take a closer look at "the relationship," what starts out as a sure bet soon turns into a qualifiedly poor candidate. The more carefully we look at "the relationship," the less of a commonality it becomes and the more apparent it is that commonalities must be described in terms that are reasonably concrete and specific.

Gelso and Carter (1985) constructed their analysis of the relationship upon Greenson's (1967) conceptualization of three interrelated relationship components: a working alliance, a transference configuration, and a "real" relationship. Gelso and Carter then show how each of these three components varies along three dimensions: (a) the extent to which a given approach regards the component as central or crucial to therapeutic change; (b) the extent to which a given approach emphasizes and counts upon the "real" relationship or the "transference" relationship; and (c) the extent to which a given approach regards the component as a means to some further end or as an end in itself. In applying this schema to humanistic, behavioral, and psychoanalytic-psychodynamic therapies, Gelso and Carter conclude that there are appreciably significant differences in the ways in which a working alliance, a transference configuration, and a real relationship figure in each of the three therapeutic families. How should the commonality be framed? Should it be framed as "the relationship" between patient and therapist, or should it be framed in the more carefully concrete and specific terms given by Gelso and Carter? If we accept the former, then we have a loosely stated commonality that is easily defended as universal. If we accept a reasonably concrete and specific framing of the commonality, then the supposed commonality tends to evaporate, to shrink to very little indeed. To qualify as genuine, the terms should be reasonably concrete and specific.

Another supposed commonality may be loosely referred to as a corrective emotional experience. Once again, this is practically tantamount to the definition of psychotherapy itself. In order to demonstrate that it is a genuine commonality, it should be framed in more concrete terms. Goldfried (1982) takes steps in this direction by describing the corrective experience as that of ". . . having patients behave in ways that they may have avoided in the past, and the accompanying realization that the consequences they feared do not, in fact, occur . . . corrective experiences, regardless of the context in which they originated, have the effect of changing the patients' or clients' views of themselves and others" (p. 17). Framed in a loose and general way as a "corrective emotional experience," experiential psychotherapy could be included among the therapies that accept the commonality. But framed in the careful way that Goldfried does, experiential psychotherapy is able to decline inclusion. Our "corrective emotional experiences" are by no means restricted to the patients behaving in ways that they may have avoided in the past. Nor is the key component seen as "realization," especially that the consequences they feared do not, in fact, occur. Finally, a yoked characteristic is not that of changing the patients' views of themselves or others.

When a commonality is framed in terms that are reasonably concrete and specific, then it is sensible to demonstrate that it does or does not suit a given therapy. When such a commonality fits a *number* of therapies, it may be accepted as genuine.

Demonstrate that therapies use the commonality under similar therapeutic conditions and to effect similar consequences. A supposed commonality is genuine to the extent that several therapies can be shown to use it under generally similar therapeutic conditions, and to effect generally similar consequences. To the extent that a supposed commonality is used under appreciably different therapeutic conditions, and also to effect appreciably different consequences, the supposed commonality is more illusory than meaningful. Consider the corrective emotional experience. Some therapies use this principle under virtually all therapeutic conditions, with virtually all patients, and in virtually all sessions. Just about every therapeutic condition is appropriate for a corrective emotional experience to be therapeutically useful. On the other hand, some therapies use this principle under a condition only when patients have suffered an early trauma and it is believed that a corrective emotional experience is the best way of resolving the damage that was done. In the same way, therapies can differ appreciably in the consequences they expect to occur. Some therapies expect that the consequence may be deep-seated personality change, whereas others may limit the expected consequences to a reduction in anxiety. If a commonality is to be accepted as genuine, it should be demonstrated that therapies use the commonality under similar conditions and to effect similar consequences.

In general, I believe that it is all but fruitless to try and integrate therapies along the lines of supposed commonalities. Yet I also believe that the strategy deserves a fair trial. If we are going to demonstrate a genuine commonality, we should (a) designate those theories of psychotherapy that share the commonality, (b) describe the commonality in terms that are reasonably concrete and specific rather than loose and general, and (c) demonstrate that therapies use the commonality under similar therapeutic conditions and to effect similar consequences. When all this is done, it can be said that the commonality is a real one.

SOME ILLUSTRATIVE COMMONALITIES

Proponents of the fifth strategy for integrating psychotherapies have identified a number of proposed commonalities. In keeping with their rationale, these commonalities fall largely under principles of therapeutic change or general therapeutic stratagems (Figure 1). If you accept these as more or less genuine commonalities across a number of psychotherapies, and if you accept the rationale that the demonstrated presence of commonalities warrants integration, then this strategy clicks into place and moves along the lines of integrating the various therapies. I am not persuaded by this rationale; but, nevertheless, what follow are some illustrative commonalities. It must be emphasized that these are merely illustrative, and therefore there is no attempt to frame them in ways that sharply distinguish one from the other. They are at somewhat different levels of abstraction, and some overlap onto others. Nevertheless, here are some illustrative commonalities.

Corrective emotional experience

From its introduction by Alexander and French (1946), many psychotherapies have been described as providing this kind of experience for the patient. As discussed above, the meaning of "corrective emotional experience" has come to include the correction of previously avoided actions, the correction of the ill effects of previous experiences, the exposing of oneself to feared situations, the taking of risks, attempting to respond in new and different ways, and so on (e.g., Goldfried, 1980, 1982b; Strupp, 1986).

The engagement of new effective behaviors

One kind of therapeutic goal and direction of change (Figure 1) involves the patient's engagement of new effective behavior. In other words, the patient is to be, behave, and act in some way that is both new and effective. This may otherwise be described as increasing the patient's repertoire of available behaviors, providing increased freedom of choice, enabling increasingly accurate information-processing, facilitating decision-making, and so on (Prochaska & DiClemente, 1982). Yet the common denominator is that the patient behaves in some new and effective way.

There are several ways of delineating the actual commonality. One way is to see the commonality as the sheer goal of the patient's engaging in new and effective behaviors. Second, the commonality may be held as residing not so much in the goal but rather in the actual in-therapy occurrence of the new and effective behaviors. Third, the commonality can be seen as residing in the means by which the behavior is understood as brought about. For example, the new and effective behavior may be said to be brought about by means of contingency management of conditioned stimuli (Prochaska & DiClemente, 1982), by means of reality testing and direct feedback (Goldfried, 1980, 1982), by means of a mixed bag of experiential operations (Mahrer, 1986a), or numberless other ways, including the postulated relationship between cognitive processes and effective performance, and the ensuing sense of mastery: "The apparent diversity of theory and practice can be reconciled by postulating that cognitive processes mediate change but that cognitive events are induced and altered most readily by experience of mastery arising from effective performance" (Bandura, 1977, p. 191).

The provision of an alternative life perspective

Another proposed commonality is that many therapies provide the patient with an alternative life perspective. Regardless of how this is brought about (i.e., the particular therapeutic stratagems), the providing of an alternative life perspective is held as a common principle of therapeutic change. It is variously described as an alternative system of values, frame of reference, personal and world philosophy, or working perspective on life (Beutler, 1983; Frank, 1973, 1982; Goldfried, 1982b; Goldfried & Padawer, 1982; Gomes-Schwartz, 1978; Marmor, 1976; Mintz, Auerbach, Luborsky, & Johnson, 1973; Orlinsky & Howard, 1977, 1978). Some contend that this is common across only a few therapies, and others hold that this is common across all therapies: ". . . all forms of therapy share a common clinical strategy of providing patients/clients with an alternative way of looking at themselves, their behavior, and the world around them" (Goldfried, 1982b, p. 16).

Therapist-patient relationship

For those who espouse this fifth strategy, the therapist-patient relationship is one of the favorite commonalities across the preponderance of therapies, if not as a characteristic of all therapies. Various aspects may be highlighted, such as the transference relationship, helping relationship, working alliance, facilitating relationship, real relationship, or encountering relationship. Regardless, the therapist-patient relationship is heralded as a common principle of therapeutic change across all or nearly all therapies. Theories may differ on how this relationship exerts its commonality. It may be that the relationship is the medium through which other effective techniques exert their influence, the means whereby the therapist serves as exemplar or role model, or the stage upon which are played out such therapist qualities as social sensitivity, ability to listen well, a genuine commitment to helping, or a solid integrity and intactness (Strupp, 1979; Wilson & Evans, 1976, 1977). Whatever the reason or whatever its variations and themes, the therapist-patient relationship is a popular proposed commonality.

Expectant readiness to social influence

Another commonality also refers to a principle of therapeutic change. Essentially, the commonality is that in many or most therapies the patient is described as being in a state of readiness for therapy. Stated more carefully, the commonalilty consists of the patient's expectant readiness that therapy will be of help (Frank, 1973; Marmor, 1976; Prochaska, 1979), and the therapist's willingness to cultivate that expectancy by means of such social influence mechanisms as providing support, persuasion, and suggestion (Frank, 1973; Marmor, 1976). So central is this principle, that many therapies consider such a patient state as necessary for psychotherapy to get started, and it is exceedingly common for many therapies to use methods aimed at placing the patient in this state of appropriate expectancy.

Consciousness-expanding self-exploration

Another popular commonality is the principle of therapeutic change by means of consciousness-expanding self-exploration. In client-centered therapy it refers to the patient's inner felt exploration of self. In psychodynamic-psychoanalytic therapies it refers to insight and self-understanding. In Gestalt therapy it refers to awareness. Therapies vary in how it is understood as working, in how to bring it about, in what aspects of the self are to be focused upon and explored, and in many other ways. Nevertheless, the commonality consists in the expanding of consciousness through the exploration of self.

These are some of the popular commonalities which are proposed as occurring across various psychotherapies. If several therapies can be shown to share one or more of these commonalities, then the strategy holds that the therapies may be integrated with one another. Since these commonalities are predominantly principles of therapeutic change, then integration may mean that change components of the sharing therapies may be adopted by one another. For example, if two or more therapies share the principle of consciousness-expanding self-exploration, then these therapies may adopt each others' general therapeutic stratagems for achieving consciousness-expanding self-exploration, or they may use this principle for achieving goals borrowed from the other therapies. In any case, these are some illustrations of commonalities along which therapies may be integrated in this fifth strategy.

CONSEQUENCES FOR THE FIELD OF PSYCHOTHERAPY

Those who are drawn toward this fifth strategy have faith that the many psychotherapies would begin a process of blending with one another once their shared commonalities have been properly illuminated. I cannot share this faith. However, if genuine commonalities can be demonstrated, then I wish the integrationists well in their efforts to blend the therapies that are truly joined together at the points of their commonalities.

Nevertheless, use of this fifth strategy will tend to have its own distinctive consequences for the field of psychotherapy. Suppose we accept the proposition that many psychotherapies have common therapeutic goals and directions of change, common principles of therapeutic change, common general therapeutic stratagems, and that these many psychotherapies are rather similar to one another in terms of effectiveness. If this proposition is generally accepted, then I foresee the following consequences.

A justified status quo

The more that therapies are accepted as being rather similar in effectiveness, the greater the number of commonalities that are accepted, and the larger the number of therapies that are included, the greater is the likelihood that therapies will tend to remain pretty much as they are. Commonalities can easily have the effect of grand levelers. If there are widespread commonalities across nearly all therapies, if differences wash away, then the juice goes out of the enterprise to enhance them. Accept the status quo. Why do research to discover ways to develop the therapy further? Why see how and where the therapy can be improved or more efficaciously applied?

One of the hungers for integrating therapies *is* the keen search for something *better*, for improving the lot of our various therapies. Why bother to integrate several therapies if they already share commonalities? The integrated product would be pretty much like the therapies that were integrated. Most of the enthusiasm is easily depleted, and the consequence is a justified status quo.

A smaller number of faceless integrative therapies

A second likely consequence is a smaller number of faceless integrative therapies. The grim likelihood is the gradual emergence of a few therapies comprised largely of integrative commonalities, a loosely organized therapeutic mush. Such therapies would likely start with the presumption that patients come with an expectancy that therapy will be helpful, and the therapies would use the relationship, self-exploration, and corrective experiences to provide a new life perspective and enable the patient to engage new behaviors. Instead of intact and identifiable therapies, the products would tend to be a few dreary, faceless, unsubstantive mélanges of loosely connected commonalities. Commonalities can be deadly!—especially as major therapeutic building blocks. The fifth strategy, however, can lead to either a smaller number of faceless integrative therapies—or a still *larger* number of highly individualized therapies.

Mushrooming proliferation

An alternative consequence is a mushrooming proliferation of therapies. Rather than an explosion of lots of good therapies, I see this as a quieter differentiation of the static status quo into myriad idiosyncratic therapies. After all, if most therapies are pretty much like all others, if commonalities abound, then *each* of us may justifiably do whatever we do. Why not? If we all share so many commonalities, then schools and approaches and theories lose their integrity. In this mushrooming proliferation each therapist would very nearly be doing his or her individual brand of therapy.

If most therapies share the same general degree of effectiveness, then this adds to the likelihood of mushrooming proliferation. If my therapy is not appreciably better or worse than your therapy, then each of us may as well do our own. If we accept a more elegant rule of looking at effectiveness in terms of which therapies are more effective in what ways with what patients with what problems, then the consequence is even more solidified. Combine that line of studying effectiveness with the proposition of widespread commonalities, and any therapy is just as good in its own way as any other therapy. Once again, we arrive at the likelihood of mushrooming proliferation.

I regard these consequences as rather unfortunate for the field of psychotherapy. I also foresee these consequences as occurring to the extent that commonalities are stated in terms that are relatively loose and general, and to the extent that the loose, general commonalities are presented as widespread across most psychotherapies. My overall reaction to this strategy is anything but enthusiastic support, nor do I look forward to the likely consequences on the field of psychotherapy.

Chapter 6

DIAGNOSE-THE-PROBLEM AND PRESCRIBE-THE-TREATMENT

The idea behind the final strategy is simple and has the advantage of face appeal. There are lots of different psychotherapies. Some are more effective than others in treating particular problems. Once you diagnose the problem, then it is sensible to select and use the best therapeutic approach for that problem. Integration means that we have a broad package of available therapies and therapeutic programs, and we select and use the most appropriate one or ones for the problem at hand.

This strategy does not involve the development of some intact, substantive new theoretical system or psychotherapy, but merely uses all or most of them as they may be appropriate for the problem. Accordingly, this strategy differs from the first one, which involves the development of substantive new theories of psychotherapy. It differs from the fourth strategy, which involves the development of an integrative new super-framework; and it differs from the fifth, which involves the integration of therapies that share commonalities. Because this sixth strategy goes well beyond the mere integration of concretely specific working therapeutic operations, and also beyond the integration of therapeutic vocabularies, it differs from the second and third strategies respectively.

WHAT THIS STRATEGY IS: THE RATIONALE

The rationale for this sixth strategy is the convergence of an old and established clinical axiom and a new formulation of a basic research question in the field of psychotherapy. Long before psychotherapies became respectable, clinicians in many professional disciplines accepted the axiom that you first diagnose the problem and then apply the appropriate treatment. It has been the traditional practice in medicine, dentistry, and other clinical professions. The first step is diagnosis, problem-identification, assessment, evaluation. Once you know what the problem is, then apply the appropriate treatment program. When psychotherapies developed, it was easy and sensible to adopt this old and established clinical axiom.

In psychotherapy research, the old clinical axiom was translated into a research axiom. So widely accepted has this formulation become that it has been acknowledged as perhaps the basic question in psychotherapy research (Parloff, 1979). Of the various formulations of this basic research question, Paul's (1967) is perhaps the most apt in setting researchers to study the question: *"What* treatment, by *whom,* is most effective for *this* individual with *that* specific problem, and under *which* set of circumstances" (p. 111). In many ways, this is a careful research wording of the clinical axiom that first you identify the problem and then apply the proper treatment program. This is the rationale.

HOW THIS STRATEGY WORKS

There are two general ways of putting this strategy to work. In one, the therapist essentially holds to no given therapeutic approach. Rather than functioning within an experiential approach or a cognitive behavioral approach or a Sullivanian approach, the therapist first identifies the problem and then selects and applies the proper treatment program from a large number of available ones. In carrying out these two steps, the therapist is an eclectic or integrative therapist rather than an experiential or cognitive behavioral or Sullivanian therapist. If the problem is a fear of crossing streets or a lack of assertiveness, an inability to cope with stress or test anxiety, a decisional conflict or a persistent headache, a marital problem or a depressive state, then there are treatment packages and approaches that are explicitly effective and appropriate for that problem, and the proper one is to be applied. The therapist rises above any particular therapeutic school or approach.

One of the purest examples of this way of using the strategy is Goldstein and Stein's prescriptive approach (1976). It consists of a comprehensive schema of therapeutic programs and procedures organized on the basis of the problems for which each has been shown to be effective. Once the patient is appropriately classified and the nature of the problem determined, then the therapist selects and applies the appropriate treatment program and procedure.

In Halgin's (1985) version of this strategy, four different therapeutic approaches are pragmatically blended and applied on the basis of the patient's determined need:

> Pragmatic blending . . . taps four theoretical models: psychodynamic, interpersonal, person-centered, and behavioral . . . it allows the therapist . . . actually encourages—to determine the course of the treatment in response to the immediate needs of the client. Direction can be provided as warranted; exploration can be done when appropriate; and support can be offered when needed . . . the pragmatic blending of approaches requires that the therapist carefully assess the client's needs and make a determination as to which aspects of varying approaches would be warranted. (p. 558)

But this is only one way of putting the strategy to work. In a second way, the therapist operates within some given therapeutic approach and then, at some point in the therapy, determines that another approach is more appropriate, and switches to the other approach. The strategy comes into play when the therapist determines that right now the patient needs what some other approach has to offer, or that the immediately emerging problem is best treated by means of some other therapeutic approach. Here is where the therapist diagnoses the emergent problem and prescribes a (different) treatment. This second way of using the strategy is perhaps most common in psychodynamic and behavioral approaches.

There are several reported cases in which a therapist following either a psychodynamic or a behavioral approach turns to the other (Bernstein, 1984; Birk, 1970; Birk & Brinkley-Birk, 1974; Brady, 1968; Feather & Rhoads, 1972). A psychodynamic-psychoanalytic therapist, after some years of working with a patient, decides that the patient's newly emergent phobias should best be treated by a desensitization approach, after which the psychodynamic-psychoanalytic treatment is to be resumed. Alternatively, a desensitization therapist reasons that the patient's emergent (transference) relationship is interfering with the patient's willingness to carry out homework assignments, opts for a period of analyzing and interpreting the (transference) relationship, and then resumes the desensitization program (cf. Cohen & Pope, 1980; Marmor, 1971; Rhoads & Feather, 1972, 1974; Weinburg & Zaslow, 1963; Weitzman, 1967). Birk (1970), for example, illustrates how bed-wetting is treated by the bell and blanket behavioral method, but if it is determined that the patient's psychodynamics around his mother are sabotaging the patient's motivation for carrying out the homework assignments, then psychodynamic interpretative procedures may be used to promote insight into the patient's passive dependency upon his mother in her interference with the homework.

In either way of using this strategy, the therapist determines that this present problem calls for application of a different treatment approach. This determination may take place in the initial sessions, during a given session, or after many sessions of following a selected therapeutic approach. Once the determination is made, the therapist then proceeds to select from one or more available treatment approaches the one deemed appropriate—and to be carried out by this or another therapist.

Critique: It Is Not Feasible to Carry Out This Strategy

I believe that it is quite feasible to determine the nature of a problem and then to do what is appropriately called for—as long as one operates within a single overarching therapeutic approach. That single approach may be an experiential approach, a rational-emotive approach, any approach at all, including a single overarching eclectic or integrative approach. However, my thesis is that it is not feasible to do this by switching from one approach to another; it is not feasible to carry out the steps of this strategy; this strategy will not work.

The strategy consists of two steps. The first is diagnosis of the problem, and the second is the prescription of an appropriate treatment. These are the two steps, whether the therapist starts out to do this in the initial sessions, or whether the therapist first works within one approach and then switches. In any case, critics hold that two different approaches cannot be combined, and that one cannot switch from one to another. Messer and Winokur (1980, 1984), Rachman (1970), and Krasner (1968) have discussed the infeasibility of switching in this way between psychodynamic and behavioral approaches. They contend that the two approaches have distinctly different theories of human beings and distinctly different theories of practice, and therefore the two approaches would have distinctly different ways of diagnosing the problem and also of prescribing the appropriate psychodynamic or behavioral treatments. I agree.

But my thesis goes even further. If we take a closer look at "diagnosing the problem," I submit that it is a complicated process consisting of a series of three steps which must be undertaken in more or less the following sequence. (a) The therapist must first decide on the nature and content of the useful material to be elicited in order to diagnose the problem. (b) Next the therapist must have a particular way of listening and observing. This involves both *how* to listen and observe the elicited material, and *what* to listen for and observe. (c) The therapist must then arrive at some higher-order description of the patient and target of change within some diagnostic framework.

This is the identified problem or difficulty or treatment target. Diagnosing the problem is the end result of these three steps (Figure 1).

Prescribing the appropriate treatment is likewise more than an automatic next step. Instead, I submit that it is the end result of the next set of steps: (d) Once the therapist arrives at the higher-order description of the patient, target of change, problem, difficulty, treatment target, the therapist must then have some therapeutic goal and direction of change, i.e., given that problem, what do you want to accomplish with regard to that problem? (e) Finally, the therapist must select some general therapeutic stratagem which is held to be effective in arriving at that therapeutic goal. In other words, these five steps comprise what is loosely described as diagnosing the problem and prescribing the treatment.

My thesis is that (a) some approach, some framework, some theory of psychotherapy is needed for each of these five steps; (b) each theory of psychotherapy will have its own distinctive way of proceeding through each of these five steps; and (c) it is infeasible and unworkable to switch from one theory of psychotherapy to another at any and all of these five steps. In summary, my thesis is that the strategy of diagnosing the problem and prescribing an appropriate treatment is infeasible and will not work.

Some approach is needed to determine the nature of the useful data for identifying the problem. Somehow the therapist arrives at a conclusion that the problem is a lack of assertiveness, or an excessive rigidity, that the patient is alcoholic, or is phobic of enclosed places, or is unable to tolerate a close relationship. Yet the framing of the problem does not simply appear. It takes some doing to elicit the proper data so that the therapist can arrive at that conclusion. The proper data may be obtained prior to therapy, at an "intake evaluation," in the initial sessions, or in the middle of the twentieth session. But whenever it *is* obtained, the therapist must have some explicit hand in eliciting the kind of data that are useful.

Suppose that the therapist arrived at a conclusion that the patient is phobic of enclosed places, or that the patient is unable to tolerate a close relationship. And suppose we ask the therapist what the data were that allowed such a determination of the problem. Whatever the therapist answers is quite likely to show the kind of data that particular therapist finds useful, and also that a particular therapeutic approach elicits such data. For example, one therapist may say, "In the beginning of the first session, I asked the patient what he considered the problem, and he said, 'I get uptight whenever I'm in an enclosed place like a car or airplane or even a crowded room. It's been driving me crazy for years. I can't get rid of it. I've tried.' " Another therapist may say, "The intake evaluation included projective tests, and the report mentioned that he may have a phobia of enclosed places." A third therapist says, "The phobia surfaced in the second year of analysis, after we were working with early material around birth trauma." Here are useful data that are elicited because the therapist trusts the central importance of "the patient's problem," concepts such as birth trauma, phobia, and the particular psychodynamic approach underlying projective tests.

These are interesting kinds of elicited data, not all of which might be invited and used in all approaches. For example, the experiential approach does not use the initial session to have the patient tell the therapist what the patient regards as the major presenting problem. Nor does the experiential approach elicit intake or pre-therapy assessments, so there would not be any projective data. Nor would the experiential approach elicit material surrounding "birth trauma" and name the material as indicating a "phobia." Indeed, there is no looking for a "problem" toward which therapeutic "treatment" is applied. Instead, the patient is shown how to allow the preponderance of attention to focus on anything that proves to be accompanied with heightened bodily sensations and experiencing. Accordingly, the patient may focus upon delightful recent changes that are front and center, a fleeting image that is fascinatingly compelling, a moment of sheer pleasure and happiness—or a painful memory, something awful that just occurred, some terrible part of the patient's very core which is tearing the patient apart. The attentional center may be that which is regarded in other approaches as a problem, but the important data consist of the nature and content of the accompanying experiencings rather than some "problem" that therapy is to "treat."

From the perspective of experiential psychotherapy, the

whole enterprise of seeking to define some problem, an enterprise so characteristic of so many psychotherapies, serves two major experiential purposes. One is that it is a means whereby the patient can gain a given kind of experiencing. The patient who says, "I don't know what to do about my marriage, cause we just don't talk anymore," or "When I have to use an elevator I just get tense as hell," is using these words as a means of gaining some kind of experiencing. It may be the experiencing of securing someone to say personal things to, or the experiencing of sheer complaining or some other experiencing. The therapeutically useful aspect is the nature of the experiencing as the patient defines and frames the problem rather than the actual content of the "problem," as grasped by some other therapeutic framework.

Second, when the therapist and patient work conjointly with one another so that the patient defines something as the problem, they are engaged in the mutual construction of defined roles and the relationships they are inclined to have between those roles. For example, the therapist is thereby defined as the one to help, to fix the problem, to make it all better, and the patient is defined as the broken one, the one who deserves and has a right to be helped. Or, by talking about "the problem" in the right way, the therapist is defined as the one with whom the patient can really be close, can be more intimate and revealing than anyone else in the patient's world, and the patient is defined as the one who craves closeness and intimacy, the one to whom such bonding is so very precious and needed.

In experiential psychotherapy, we do not need information that serves as the data for identifying the problem. For most other approaches, however, "the problem" is their essential justification, and therefore it is necessary to decide on the kind of information to be elicited in order to define the problem.

Each therapeutic approach has its own set of data that it accepts as useful, and whatever data that has been elicited has occurred by following some given therapeutic approach. In gathering data useful for arriving at an identification of the problem, you may emphasize neurological test data, information provided by a referral source, case history information, patient self-report, material from recent or recurrent or remote dreams, the therapist's psychodiagnostic impressions, the therapist's inferences about the irrational ideas, the problem as articulated by the patient in the initial sessions, and on and on. There are hundreds of pieces of information to select from, and each approach makes its own distinctive selection of information which it uses as data in its own distinctive way.

Do eclectic-integrative therapies assemble all the relevant data from all the various approaches in order to move toward a diagnosis of the problem? That is just not possible; the answer is no, they cannot. When we suggest that each approach determines its own data useful for identifying the problem, does this apply to eclectic-integrative approaches? I believe that the answer is yes, i.e., everything starts with the kind of data you elicit, and each approach elicits its own kind of data.

One of the most accepted eclectic approaches has been developed by Beutler (1983). What kinds of data does this eclectic approach elicit in order to move toward a framing of the problem? In Beutler's approach, the therapist gathers quite selectively explicit data on (a) the complexity of the symptoms. This ranges from simple habits "reinforced but relatively non-generalized through discriminative learning" (p. 38), to those "whose associations to the early learning pattern is very unclear" (p. 39). The therapist also gathers data on (b) the patient's "reactance potential" which "refers to an individual's investment in maintaining personal control and freedom, as is described by one's unwillingness to comply with external constraints" (p. 39). Finally, the therapist elicits data on (c) the patient's coping style. An internal coping style is one in which the patient "approaches conflict resolution by becoming preoccupied with his own internal imaginations" (p. 41); the patient uses an external coping style "by projecting blame or displacing conflict outwardly" (p. 41). Clearly, eclectic approaches do not organize all the kinds of data which all other approaches find useful to elicit in working toward the framing of a problem. Instead, each eclectic approach makes its own selection of whatever it uniquely regards as useful data. With more eclectic approaches we will only increase the number of approaches which elicit their own kinds of useful data.

Each approach will elicit its own kind of useful data which

are to be used in arriving at a statement of the problem. Each approach invites its own material, has its own ways of eliciting this material, trusts its own kind of data for processing into its own statement of "the problem." Before the therapist identifies the problem as the patient's inability to tolerate a close relationship, some given approach has been hard at work gathering some kind of useful information, on the basis of which the problem will later be formulated. There is no "problem." There is only this particular approach that uses these particular data as useful in the eventual construction of what it refers to as "the problem."

Each approach has its own way of listening to and observing the data it elicits for identifying the problem. Each approach will elicit the particular kind of data it uses for arriving at a statement of the problem. But long before arriving at that statement of the problem, each approach will listen to, observe, and make sense of the elicited data in its own way. If you are an experiential, a Jungian, or a cognitive behavioral therapist, you will listen to and observe in your own distinctive way to whatever you distinctively invited the patient to say and do on your way toward arriving at your distinctive statement of the problem.

Let us revert to the patient saying, "I get uptight whenever I'm in an enclosed place like a car or an airplane or even a crowded room. It's been driving me crazy for years. I can't get rid of it. I've tried." One therapist may listen for the nature of the experiencing that is present as the patient says these words in whatever way they are said. An experiential therapist may "hear" a sense of utter helplessness, an experiencing of giving in, of being defeated, of surrender. Another therapist may observe by being vigilant of attentional splits, and this therapist notices the clenched fist as the patient says, "It's been driving me crazy . . ." A third therapist listens with special sensitivity to the symbolic meanings with regard to the immediate therapist-patient relationship, and is therefore attuned to the implied meanings slanted toward an overpowering, suffocating therapist-patient relationship. A fourth therapist listens psychodiagnostically, and is developing inferences about the patient's phobic or possibly schizoid or borderline condition. Here are four fine therapists, each listening in a most distinctive way, and each able to justify that way as correct, accurate, and right.

Even when therapists listen to and observe the same material that is supposed to contain the problem, each approach will enable its therapists to have their own distinctive way of listening to and observing the material (Mahrer, 1980, 1983a; Mahrer & Gervaize, 1983; Mahrer & Pearson, 1973; Silverman, 1974). Messer (1986) acknowledges this difference in a general way: ". . . eclectics share one particular philosophical outlook on the best way to view psychologica data, while adherents of specific schools prefer others" (p. 384). The philosophical outlook of how to view the data refers to how to listen to and observe what you invite the patient to say and do. I suggest that there are sharp differences across all schools of psychotherapy, including all integrative and eclectic schools of psychotherapy.

Not only does each approach have its own way of listening to and observing the elicited material, but approaches differ even in labeling that material as containing or not containing the problem. A somewhat extreme example is that of experiential psychotherapy where what the patient says and does is regarded as meaningful only when the patient's attention is predominantly on something personal, rather than spoken mainly to the therapist, and when the patient's words and behaviors are accompanied with a moderate level of experiencing. Dead and neutral speech, without feeling and experiencing, is not accepted as therapeutically meaningful. Regardless of the content of the statement, if it is experientially dead, the material is therapeutically meaningless. If there is no feeling, if experiential listening leaves the therapist with neutral, dead, flat experiencing, it does not matter what the patient is saying: "I am an alcoholic; that is my problem . . ." "I wish I could leave my home to be with people, but I only leave home maybe once a week because I am so scared . . ." "My problem is that I am a mass murderer, and I have killed 114 people in three provinces . . ." If these words are experientially dead, the experiential therapist does not listen and observe in such a way as to conclude that the patient's problem is alcoholism, or being scared to leave home, or mass murdering.

Experiential psychotherapy is an extreme example because it restricts itself to experientially loaded patient statements, and also because the therapist does not listen so as to formulate some sort of "problem." But even therapies that find the notion of identifying the problem as appealing have guidelines for accepting given statements as containing something about the problem. Are the words "I am an alcoholic" spoken flippantly, challengingly, defiantly, hopelessly, tensely, secretively? Are they said after the patient has tearfully recounted the awful incident of having driven from the scene after hitting the child who is still in the hospital recovering from severe head injuries? Even with approaches that salute the idea of identifying a problem, it is not all that easy to listen and observe in such a way as to label that particular material as containing the right data for identifying the problem.

Arriving at a statement of the problem means first eliciting the right material from the patient, and then listening and observing in such a way that you can say, here is the problem. Once you elicit the kind of material you like to use, you must then take some approach to listen to and observe the material. Whichever approach you use may hear that statement as containing a problem or as not containing a problem. Whichever approach you use will likely make its own unique sense of the material that is listened to and observed. What is more, there should be no switching away from the step of eliciting the material you wish to listen and observe. If you use a neurological approach in eliciting the data, it is highly unlikely that you will listen to and observe the material from a psychoanalytic approach. If you seek to elicit the useful material by means of the patient's free associations, it is not really feasible to listen to and observe the flow of free associations from a rational-emotive vantage point. Eliciting the problem-relevant material, and listening to and observing that elicited material, are almost inevitably done within some single given, consistent approach. There can hardly be any switching here.

It sounds appealing to say that first you diagnose the problem and then prescribe the treatment. But it is not feasible to do this. You must operate within some approach in determining and eliciting whatever data you regard as useful in determining the problem. Furthermore, once you elicit whatever data you choose, you must listen to and observe those data within some given approach, and each approach has its own way of carrying out this basic and sensitive step. Yet the difficulties do not stop here.

Framing of the problem

The framing or diagnosing of the problem is, according to our thesis, the outcome of a rather complicated process involving both patient and therapist, an achievement that requires the consistent use of some explicit or implicit approach, and that cannot be accomplished by combining or switching different approaches.

In the actual framing of the problem, one way is for the therapist to leave the job in the hands of the patient. That is, it is the patient who frames the problem and defines the content to be changed, while it is the therapist whose job it is to apply the appropriate treatment for that problem. This position is exemplified by Prochaska and DiClemente (1982):

> The client can initially serve as the expert on the content
> to be changed while the therapist serves as the expert on
> the processes that can produce change. (p. 282)

I accept that the therapist is the expert on the processes that can produce change. However, the client's naming of this as the problem, as the content to be changed, is the culmination of a complex process in which the therapist is a very active and involved determinant. It is the therapist who plays a very large hand in inviting the client to attend to "the problem" rather than some other material, in inviting the client to provide this or that kind of data, in eliciting the kind of information which includes the "content to be changed." Therapist and client work together in eliciting the data that are regarded as useful in identifying the problem. The therapist actively participates in listening to the information in whatever way leads to the particular way of framing the problem. The therapist is an active participant in all the steps that culminate in the actual framing of the problem. It is quite likely that in initial sessions the patient's statement of "the content to be changed" will vary considerably from a rational-emotive therapist to a feminist therapist to a psychoanalytic therapist to a family therapist to a bioenergetic therapist. The therapist is in no way a passive nonparticipant in the patient's framing of the "content to be changed." By the time the patient has specified the content to be changed, the therapist has played a very large and conjointly determining hand.

Consider the extreme situation in which it is the very beginning of the initial session. Suppose that this opening segment is studied by a number of therapists representing a number of different therapeutic approaches, and that they all agree that they will try and frame the problem from something the patient says in the beginning of the session. Forget that each approach would likely elicit different material so that this sentence would be elicited only by some of the approaches. Let us only consider the patient saying, "I get uptight whenever I'm in an enclosed place like a car or an airplane or even a crowded room. It's been driving me crazy for years. I can't get rid of it. I've tried." Picture that the patient is saying these words in earnest. He is not bawling his head off and beating his head against a wall. He is not whispering so that the therapist cannot hear. He is not aggressively eyeball-to-eyeball with the therapist. He is just saying these words in simple direct fashion.

Even under these extreme conditions, the framing of "the problem" will vary with the approach, for each approach will listen to and observe the meaningful material distinctly. One may frame the problem as anxiety in enclosed places such as cars, airplanes, and crowded rooms. A second therapist may frame the problem as a phobic condition with perhaps some schizoid or borderline features. An experiential therapist may attend to the experiencing of helplessness, giving in, being defeated. Another therapist, observing the clenched fist with the words, "It's driving me crazy," may frame the problem as a splitting off of energy tied to aggression. Other therapists may frame the problem as the patient's anxiety about entering into therapy and into the imminent therapist-patient relationship.

Even with the same single sentence, spoken in the beginning of the initial session, there is plenty of room for quite different ways of listening to and observing what the patient says and does, and then arriving at a distinctive way of framing whatever is taken as the problem.

But all of this presumes that in each approach the patient would say the same sentence, and that all approaches concur that the problem is somehow contained in the same agreed-upon single sentence. And that almost never is the case. One important reason that it is almost never the case is that each approach will tend to elicit its own kind of material which is then to be used to frame the problem.

Furthermore, the problem is rarely gift-wrapped in a single sentence. In pre-therapy intake evaluations, in initial sessions, and certainly in subsequent sessions, the problem is arrived at from dozens and dozens of sentences. If we listen to two or three consecutive sessions, it is easy to agree that what the patient actually says and does is indeed a function of the approach used by the therapist. But even so, the framing of the problem calls for a complicated process of selection and organization from a great deal of words and behaviors coming from the patient. Once we study two or three consecutive sessions, it begins to become clear that approaches will differ markedly in how they select, organize, listen to, and finally arrive at a statement of the problem. Indeed, some approaches may even abstain because the information elicited by the actual therapist is not the kind needed by the approach that is trying to arrive at some framing of the problem.

The matter becomes even more complicated when more and more material in the rest of the session and in all the subsequent sessions begins to pile up. It may appear that the problem was that the patient is anxious in enclosed places, as he said in the first session. But by the fourth session, he rarely even mentioned that. Instead, he seems to be complaining bitterly about his brother-in-law, the brother-in-law's wife, and their two children, living with them for the past 2 months. He also is mentioning that sometimes he gets headaches and cannot sleep, and he talks about the increasing arguments with his wife. As all the new topics tumble over one another, how does the ther-

apist put all of this together in framing or reframing whatever
is to be regarded as the problem by the middle of the fourth
session? Indeed, the framing of "the problem" is a most complicated process in which the therapist seems to be a very active
determinant.

We have now arrived at a point where a therapist pro-
claims that the problem is the patient's alcoholism, or that the
patient is phobic of enclosed places, or that the patient is unable to tolerate a close relationship. I submit, first, that this is a
complicated achievement of at least three interrelated steps, each
of which almost requires that the therapist stay within some
given therapeutic approach. It cannot be done by somehow es-
caping from some therapeutic approach or by universal consensus. Second, I submit that the identifying of a given
statement of the problem is more or less unique to that approach, and cannot be achieved by combining different approaches, and certainly not by switching from one approach to
another in the course of the steps culminating in the framing
of the problem. In other words, diagnosing and framing the
problem is infeasible and unworkable in this strategy. It is illusory to try to find "the problem" as if it exists outside some quite
explicit approach. By the time you have framed the problem,
you have engaged in a sophisticated set of steps, all drenched
in some very particular approach.

Setting the therapeutic goal and direction of change

Once you diagnose the problem, the strategy sounds as if
you automatically jump to prescribing the appropriate treatment. But that is not the way it works. First you have to set some
therapeutic goal and direction of change. How do you proceed
from saying that here is the diagnosed problem to arriving at
some therapeutic goal and the welcomed direction of change?

In many therapeutic approaches, once you diagnose the
problem, the approach will have some built-in way of arriving
at an appropriate goal and direction of change. Indeed, the very
words used to specify the problem imply the goal and direction
of change. For example, suppose the problem is specified as
"lack of adequate control over aggressive impulses." The vir-

tually built-in goal is for the patient to gain "adequate" control over aggressive impulses. However, if the same patient is instead described as having a problem of petit mal seizures, manifested by myoclonic contractions of the flexor muscles and akinetic attacks with muscular hypotonia, then there is a different built-in therapeutic goal, for example, the reduction of the petit mal seizures and the accompanying symptomatology. The approach determines what words are used to frame the problem, and these words in turn imply the therapeutic goal. Word the problem as a phobia of enclosed places, alcoholism, inability to tolerate a close relationship, and the built-in therapeutic goal is that the patient no longer has a phobia of enclosed places, is no longer alcoholic, is able to tolerate a close relationship.

Proceeding from a statement of the problem to a setting of the therapeutic goal and direction of change is more or less automatic when the problem is stated in particular terms that typically contain a built-in therapeutic goal and direction of change. It also means there is little or no room here for switching approaches. One approach defines the problem, and the same approach builds in the therapeutic goal and direction of change.

What about problems that are apparently stated in more or less neutral terms wherein the therapeutic goal and direction of change are not so clearly built in? Consider the stating of a problem as the presence of latent homosexuality in a married man, or aggressive tendencies in a gentle and quiet woman. Before prescribing a treatment program, what would be the therapeutic goal and direction of change? The answer is not so clear. There is some latitude when problems are stated like this. For many problems framed in this manner, it becomes rather clear that between the diagnosis of the problem and the prescribing of an appropriate treatment, there really is an intermediate step of setting some therapeutic goal and direction of change. If the therapeutic goal and direction of change are set at getting rid of the man's maladjustive homosexual impulses so that he can lead a normal heterosexual life, the therapist may be following one approach. In different approaches, however, for a problem worded in the same way, the therapeutic goal and direction of change may be for the man to become much more comfortable with his own homosexual tendencies or to accept an avowedly homosexual life or to lead a happy life comprised of both homosexuality and heterosexuality. No matter what therapeutic goal and direction of change are set in place, some therapeutic approach is at work, and whatever approach is used makes a big difference in what treatment program is selected to do the job.

It is infeasible and unworkable to switch approaches in this step. If you are a psychoanalytic therapist in the middle of the 187th session, and you determine that the therapeutic goal and direction of change will be for the patient to gain career guidance test data regarding dairy farming, you may indeed have switched therapeutic approaches. But I doubt that you would abandon psychoanalytic therapeutic goals and directions of change for those of a career guidance approach at this point, nor would a career guidance counselor likely to have spent 187 hours doing psychoanalytic therapy. Therapeutic goals and directions of change have a way of being relatively consistent with whatever approach has been followed up to this point.

On the other hand, there are some therapies that are characterized by the same therapeutic goals and directions of change, regardless of the problem. Extreme examples are those therapies where all patients are to become more assertive, or some feminist therapies where all patients are to become freer of their cultural and traditional female roles, join the sisterhood, and contribute to the personal and political advancement of women. Some proponents of psychoanalysis apply more or less uniform therapeutic goals and directions of change to all patients. Regardless of presenting problems, the goal is the wholesale reconstruction of the character:

> . . . the goal of psychoanalysis is more ambitious than that of any other form of psychological therapy. The goal of psychodynamic therapy other than psychoanalysis is usually to overcome a symptom that has brought the patient to therapy, whereas the goal of psychoanalysis is no less than the reconstruction of character, not only to overcome symptoms but to attain as effective a level of functioning as is possible. (Gill, 1984, p. 183)

In these therapies there is no diagnosis of the problem followed by selection of an appropriate treatment from a number of available treatments. There is only one all-purpose therapeutic goal and direction of change, and one all-purpose treatment. But these therapies are exceptions to the sixth strategy.

In general, the same therapeutic approach that has worked to arrive at the statement of the problem also is at work identifying the therapeutic goal and direction of change. The identifying of the therapeutic goal and direction of change is not some theory-free step; it is done within some explicit or implicit theoretical approach. Accordingly, there is no switching of therapeutic approaches here. Some approach has set the stage for what the selected therapeutic stratagem is to accomplish.

Selecting and using the appropriate treatment stratagem

It is at this step that the strategy clicks into operation. The idea is that the therapist has diagnosed the problem and is now set to select the most appropriate treatment for the problem. The rationale for this sixth strategy accepts two ways of doing this. In one, the therapist is not supposed to operate within any given therapeutic approach. Instead, the therapist merely diagnoses the problem and then selects whatever treatment program is most appropriate for that problem. Typically, the therapist is to arrive at some identification of the problem in the beginning of therapy, and then goes about selecting which treatment is best for that problem. The advantage of the strategy is that it can call upon any or all therapeutic programs to best treat the problem. In the second way of using this strategy, the therapist does operate within some approach. For example, the therapist carries out psychodynamic therapy for a while. Then some problem presents itself in the psychodynamic therapy, and the therapist adopts the sixth strategy by selecting a treatment program outside the approach that has been used up to this point. For example, the psychodynamic therapist chooses a behavioral therapeutic stratagem as most appropriate for the problem that has surfaced in the course of the psychodynamic therapy.

My aim is to discuss each of these two conditions and to defend the thesis that this strategy is essentially infeasible and unworkable. Let us consider the first condition in which the strategy holds that the therapist is essentially free of any given therapeutic approach in diagnosing the problem and then selecting the appropriate treatment program from a broad range of available treatment programs.

To begin with, our discussion so far has argued that a therapist cannot simply note or see or diagnose a problem. By the time the therapist has framed a problem in a way that allows for a reasonable selection of a treatment stratagem, the therapist has gone through a sophisticated process of determining the nature of the elicited informational data useful for identifying the problem, has used some implicit or explicit way of listening to and observing the particular informational data that have been elicited, and has followed some approach in the particular way of framing the problem. Far from being theory-free, far from being outside of any approach, the process is drenched in some highly explicit or implicit therapeutic approach. The therapist who says that the problem is obvious, anyone can see it, is correct—as long as the others use the same approach as the therapist. So the first part of the strategy just does not hold.

What about the step of selecting the appropriate treatment stratagem for the defined problem? According to the strategy, the therapist is free to select the best treatment from a broad range of available therapies and therapeutic stratagems. Not true. If we pretend that there are 50 different treatment stratagems available from virtually all therapies, is the therapist *really* free to select the best for the problem? To begin with, the above discussion suggested that the particular framing of the problem exerts powerful pressures on the number and kind of treatment stratagems that are appropriate. By the time the therapist has gone through all the steps of framing what the therapist regards as the problem, most of the available therapeutic stratagems have been excluded, and the ones left are those cordial to whatever approach was used to arrive at that framing of the problem. But then the therapist also must choose on the basis of some more or less defined therapeutic goal and direction of change. The framing of the problem is followed by some implicit or explicit therapeutic goal and direction of change. That means the reduced range of available therapeutic stratagems is truncated even more to the very few that are effective in achieving the particular therapeutic goals and directions of change. In effect, there is virtually no leeway, no freedom to select from some presumed broad range of treatments. It is infeasible and unworkable to go outside the quite narrow set of treatment stratagems that fit the built-in therapeutic goals and directions of change. The range of selection is reduced to those that are cordially consistent with whatever therapeutic approach has been at work all along. All the therapist is doing is diagnosing the problem and selecting the appropriate treatment stratagems within some explicit or implicit therapeutic approach that has been at work from the outset. This is not an integrative strategy. I submit that this strategy is illusory, masking whatever approach the therapist has been using all along.

Let us turn to the second condition in which this strategy is presumed to be applicable. It is the condition in which a therapist works within one approach for a while and then, when some particular problem presents itself, the therapist goes outside that approach to select a more effective and appropriate treatment for that problem. If we take a closer look at this second condition, the same thesis will be defended, namely that the strategy is infeasible and unworkable.

Consider a therapist who uses a psychodynamic approach up to a point where the patient manifests a problem around anxiety when studying, and then selects a modified version of Wolpe's desensitization program as the appropriate treatment (cf. Bernstein, 1984). Suppose that the psychodynamic therapist, in one session, elicits information, that the patient, a student, was having increasing anxiety about studying for an examination. This might well occur in either a psychodynamic approach or in Wolpe's desensitization approach. At this point, the therapist listens in such a way as to frame a problem, and the problem is described as consisting of dysfunctional anxiety around studying.

Has the therapist switched from a psychodynamic to a sensitization approach right here? I would suggest that a desensitization therapist might easily label that information, about having increasing anxiety about studying, as a problem calling for desensitization treatment. I would also suggest that a desensitization therapist might easily frame the problem as dysfunctional anxiety around studying for an examination. But I am not impressed that the psychodynamic approach would seize on that information and turn it into a problem to be treated, nor that the psychodynamic approach would frame the problem as dysfunctional anxiety around studying for an examination. Instead, my impression is that the psychodynamic approach might more likely use information of the patient's increasing anxiety about studying in the same general way that most other information is used in the psychodynamic approach. I doubt that the psychodynamic approach would declare that here is a problem of dysfunctional anxiety around studying for an examination, a problem that calls for the most effective program for treatment, and outside of a psychodynamic treatment approach.

How is it that at this particular moment in the session one psychodynamic therapist elicits just that precise data from the patient, and listens in just that way to allow the therapist to conclude that here is a new problem to be described as dysfunctional anxiety around studying, a problem that calls for desensitization treatment? I suggest that the therapist has not switched from a thoroughgoing psychodynamic approach to a desensitization approach. Instead, I suggest that the therapist is already and continuously operating within some framework that is not simply psychodynamic, but rather one that allows the therapist to elicit just that particular data, to listen in just that particular way, and to frame the problem in just that way. In other words, I submit that the therapist is already operating within some modified framework. In order to effect the so-called switch from psychodynamic to desensitization, the therapist is operating within some approach that includes elements of both psychodynamic and of desensitization therapies. And if this is so, then the sixth strategy is not at play here. Selecting and using some appropriate treatment stratagem (e.g., desensitization) are not carried out within the sixth strategy. Indeed, the whole idea of so-called switching from one approach to another is, I believe, an illusion that masks the overall and continued use of some modified approach; and this is *not* the use of the sixth strategy. But let us follow the therapist in the next step.

The therapist then identifies the treatment goal as the patient's being able to study for the examination without the impairing dysfunctional anxiety. This is what some therapeutic stratagem is to accomplish, and it is a goal that is quite at home in a desensitization approach. It flows quite naturally from identifying the problem as the patient's dysfunctional anxiety around studying for an examination. I have real doubts that a psychodynamic approach would use the patient's indicating the presence of anxiety about studying for an exam to look for some therapeutic stratagem to accomplish a goal of enabling the patient to study for the examination without impairing dysfunctional anxiety. It appears that this therapeutic goal is generated by the desensitization approach rather than by the psychodynamic approach the therapist had earlier been following. It begins to look more and more that a desensitization-cordial approach has been in place all along, well before the treatment was selected.

Now the therapist chooses a therapeutic stratagem to do the job. The sixth strategy says that we just choose the best therapeutic program for the job, and the idea is that there are lots of potential candidates while only a few are best. In actuality, the problem is *already* framed in a desensitization framework, the therapeutic goal is one *already* meaningful in a desensitization framework, and the choice of desensitization is hardly a surprising one. In other words, by framing the problem and the therapeutic goal in a desensitization framework, the job has already been predetermined to go to a desensitization therapeutic stratagem.

None of this involves the sixth strategy. In fact, there never was any place for the sixth strategy throughout the whole process. Even if the therapist can be shown to have switched from a psychodynamic to a desensitization approach in eliciting the informational data, framing the problem, and identifying the therapeutic goal and direction of change, then the selected therapeutic stratagem will be one out of the desensitization approach. Nowhere has the therapist selected an appropriate treatment program from a large number of potential candidates representing various approaches. The sixth strategy never had a chance.

Indeed, my thesis is that the sixth strategy is generally infeasible and unworkable. At a superficial first look, it easily gives the impression of systematic rigor, the model of what psychotherapy can achieve, the exemplar of the science of psychotherapy. Consider the extreme and rare instance in which the patient presents a single problem that virtually all approaches accept, a problem that has a built-in therapeutic goal that all approaches accept, and where therapy involves no other major, minor, subsequent problem whatsoever. I have never come across such an instance, although I am sure that one might be found. Yet I doubt if this constitutes a sufficient proportion of cases even to justify a sixth strategy.

What is much more likely is that those therapists who seek to follow this strategy will each follow it in a uniquely idiosyncratic series of decisions resulting in a bewildering number of distinctive uses of the same overall strategy. It is a superficially rigorous, scientific schema that degenerates into lots of different therapies going in lots of different directions. Consider a patient who is seen for 10 or 30 or 120 sessions. Consider that a large group of therapists observe the patient, in the first few minutes of the first few sessions, talking in such a manner that they all agree this patient is stuttering and is quite unhappy with the stuttering. From that point on, each therapist would almost assuredly proceed in quite different directions, each one following the sixth strategy. One therapist might begin by using standard speech therapy methods such as voluntary stuttering and cancellation procedures. In the second session, the therapist focuses upon the patient's extreme anxiety around the stuttering, and elects to use a behavioral approach to reduce the anxiety. By a few sessions later, the therapist is dealing with the patient's resistance to the behavioral assignments and chooses to use psychodynamic methods to deal with this. But now the family is understood as intrusive, and the therapist elects to use family therapy methods to bring in and work with the family. By the time the therapist has gone through 10 or 30 or 120 sessions, the therapist has undertaken hundreds and hundreds of highly idiosyncratic decisions, not merely in diagnosing the next emergent problem and selecting the appropriate treatment stratagem, but in the five steps involved in each instance of selecting the next appropriate treatment stratagem.

In actual therapeutic work, the likelihood of a number of therapists carrying out this strategy in the same way over a whole series of sessions is about that of a number of chess players carrying out the same sequence of moves across a series of matches. Far from a more or less rigorous strategy, the use of this sixth strategy would more likely be license for a very large number of quite different ways of doing psychotherapy.

In summary, the strategy of diagnosing-the-problem and prescribing-the-treatment is infeasible and unworkable. It is infeasible and unworkable as a general strategy, and also when one seeks to switch from one approach to another. For those therapists who believe they are diagnosing the problem and then prescribing one best treatment from among many candidates, I submit that you are really working within some defined or undefined single approach throughout, rather than following the sixth strategy. For those who believe they follow one approach, come across a problem, and select the best of many treatments for that problem, I suggest that (a) you are instead operating within some third approach that includes elements of both, and (b) the potential treatment candidates are really a narrow few, all falling within the same consistent therapeutic approach. For those who believe this sixth strategy is rigorously scientific, I suggest that the net result will likely be that of an unsystematic proliferation of idiosyncratic uses of this sixth strategy. In any case, the strategy of diagnosing the problem and then prescribing the treatment is infeasible and unworkable.

CONSEQUENCES FOR THE FIELD OF PSYCHOTHERAPY

While I hold that this strategy is infeasible and unworkable, I am also convinced that it has a great deal of face appeal, and that many therapists are and will be attracted to this general strategy. Therefore, it seems that attempts to use this strategy will exert a number of consequences on the field of psychotherapy. In all, I believe that the consequences on the field of psychotherapy will be mixed, and will include the following:

A further differentiation between "problem treatment" psychother-

apies and "person change" psychotherapies. The overwhelming preponderance of therapists regard psychotherapy as a means of treating some problem. Diagnose the problem. Define and identify the problem. Treat the problem. Those who are attracted to the sixth strategy are "problem treatment" psychotherapists. The patient has a problem, and therapy is a good way of doing something about the problem. As proponents use this strategy more and more, there will be a further differentiation between this way of seeing psychotherapy as contrasted with psychotherapies that are designed to bring about a foundational change in the person himself or herself. In these therapies, the important locus of change is in the very core or personality of the person rather than merely in the designated problem. Indeed, there may or may not be any designated problem. If one is designated, the aim still is to allow significant change in the person, and the problem will no longer be a problem; but more importantly, the person is now a changed *person.* If there is no designated problem, these therapies still proceed with the process of change in the personality of the person, in whom and what the person is and can be.

Experiential therapy aims at enabling deep-seated changes in the person one is. So do client-centered, psychoanalytic, and 5 some other psychotherapies. For these therapies, the whole basis of the sixth strategy is alien, for the therapy is not a treatment for a problem. On the other hand, most behavioral and many psychodynamic and other therapies exist as means of treating some designated problem. The more the sixth strategy develops, the greater will be the differentiation between the therapies that enable deep-seated personality change in the person, and the therapies that provide treatment for the designated problem.

A greater emphasis on the effectiveness of given therapeutic programs in treating designated problems. As this strategy develops, it will foster greater emphasis on the effectiveness of given therapeutic programs in the treatment of designated problems. The strategy will exert pressure on designating problems to be treated, and on assessing the comparative efficacy of various programs in treating those problems. This would likely be welcomed by those who adhere to the sixth strategy, and resisted as alien and unwelcome by those who do not accept the sixth strategy. I do not accept this strategy, and I would regard as unfortunate the widespread adoption of its emphasis on demonstrated efficacy in treating designated problems.

An increase in breadth of treatment stratagems for approaches that accept this strategy. I foresee that those approaches accepting idea of designating the problem and prescribing the treatment will adopt a broader range of treatment stratagems. For example, I foresee that many behavioral approaches will borrow, modify, and adopt a fair number of psychodynamic therapeutic stratagems in their repertoire. In the same way, I expect that many psychodynamic therapists will borrow, modify, and adopt some behavioral therapeutic stratagems. I expect that the therapeutic stratagems will be modified so as to be incorporated into the existing approaches. Accordingly, the net result will be increased breadth of therapeutic stratagems in many therapeutic approaches, with each borrowing from the others. This I look forward to as good for the field of psychotherapy.

The demise of the "standard intake evaluation." It is almost accepted practice that the initial phase include a more or less standard intake evaluation in which the problem is identified and relevant background information obtained. The strategy of diagnosing the problem and prescribing the treatment goes hand-in-glove with a standard intake evaluation. If this strategy is regarded as infeasible and unworkable, I sincerely hope that one of the consequences is a demise of the standard intake evaluation, or at least the restriction of this procedure to those approaches that support the strategy. As we take increasingly closer looks at the actual steps that precede the identifying of a problem, and as we increasingly acknowledge the sharp differences among approaches at each step in this process, I hope that the standard intake evaluation will be reduced to a highly limited procedure for those approaches that are friendly.

An increase in number of therapeutic approaches. Several considerations point toward the likely increase in the sheer number of therapeutic approaches, as a consequence of this sixth strategy. One consideration is that diagnosing a problem and prescribing a treatment is the application of some implicit or explicit approach. It is not a mechanical, theory-free process.

Each way of diagnosing a problem and prescribing a treatment constitutes yet another therapeutic approach. A second consideration is that there are almost endless variations on how therapists proceed through these steps and switch from one series of steps to another. The almost inevitable consequence is a mushrooming proliferation of working approaches. I regard this as unfortunate for the field of psychotherapy.

Chapter 7

CONCLUSIONS AND RECOMMENDATIONS

We began by asking three questions: What are the various meanings and strategies for integrating psychotherapies? Which meanings and strategies are useful and workable, and which are much less so? What are the consequences for the field of psychotherapy of pursuing these strategies? We are now ready to answer these questions. These answers are the conclusions to be drawn from our discussion of the meanings and strategies.

On the basis of these conclusions, a number of recommendations are proposed. These are presented as action proposals. Because this book is for those of you are are psychotherapists—practitioners, students, teachers, and clinical researchers of psychotherapy—I am expressly inviting each of you to consider seriously each of these recommendations, and to correspond with me. Give me your reactions, your thoughts and ideas about these recommendations and about your own additional recommendations.

CONCLUSIONS

1. What are the various strategies for integrating psychotherapies?

I propose the framing of six different strategies: (a) *The integrative development of substantively new theories of psychotherapeutic practice.* By means of sound guidelines of theory construction, substantively new theories of psychotherapy are developed from modified theories of human beings, and these new theories of psychotherapy serve as integrating frameworks for those psychotherapies sharing the same parental theory of human beings. (b) *The integration of concretely specific working therapeutic operations.* A given theory of psychotherapy uses concretely specific working therapeutic operations from several different therapeutic approaches. (c) *The integration of therapeutic vocabularies.* Terms from different therapeutic approaches are integrated by demonstrating that they essentially refer to the same or similar therapeutic events; or, therapeutic vocabularies are integrated into a single overall mother language. (d) *The integrative super-framework.* A given theory of psychotherapy seeks to integrate virtually all extant theories of psychotherapy. (e) *Integrating commonalities across psychotherapies.* Several psychotherapies are integrated by identifying and using their shared commonalities. (f) *Diagnose-the-problem and prescribe-the-treatment.* After diagnosing the problem, theories are integrated by prescribing the appropriate effective treatment from a comprehensive pool of the various psychotherapies.

2. In terms of integrating psychotherapies, which strategies are useful and workable and which are much less so?

I propose that two and a half strategies are useful and workable in integrating psychotherapies. One consists of developing substantively new theories of psychotherapy from a parent theory of human beings. This will succeed in integrating those psychotherapies sharing the same parental theory of human beings. A second consists of developing a large pool of concretely specific operating procedures. Each theory then adopts new operating procedures into its repertoire through soft or hard clinical study. The half strategy is that of integrating therapeutic vocabularies by means of the "little meaning." That is, a measure of integration among vocabularies can be achieved by identifying words and terms in different therapies that share the same referent events. I propose that these are the two and a half strategies that are useful and workable in achieving these two and a half different meanings of the "integration of psychotherapies."

On the other hand, I suggest that three and a half other strategies are not useful or workable for integrating psychotherapies. One of these is the strategy of trying to elevate one approach into the super-framework that is supposed to integrate all or most others. This strategy depends largely upon merchandizing and competitive muscle. A second is the postulating of commonalities across approaches, and the elevating of a given approach as best incorporating the selected commonalities. The third strategy is to diagnose the problem and then prescribe a treatment stratagem from a range of available treatment stratagems. The additional half strategy is that of trying to integrate psychotherapeutic vocabularies by developing a grand mother tongue, a common vocabulary for all psychotherapies. I propose that these three and a half strategies are much less useful and workable. I propose that these three and a half meanings of integrating psychotherapies be regarded as essentially useless and unworkable.

When you think of useful and workable meanings of integration, and strategies for getting at these meanings, think of the two and a half former ones. When you think of meanings and strategies that are useless and unworkable, think of the three and a half latter ones.

3. What are the consequences for the field of psychotherapy of pursuing these strategies?

Depending on which strategies are pursued, our analysis suggests that there will be quite different but quite strong consequences on the field of psychotherapy. Here are three prominent consequences:

A small number of sound, distinctive psychotherapies. Instead of so very many therapeutic approaches, there will be a much smaller number of perhaps five or ten or so. The added bonus is that these theories of psychotherapy would likely be both broader and sounder than most of those we have now. In the course of this line of developing integration, it is likely that we will become much more sophisticated in spelling out our theories of psychotherapy, in locating and strengthening areas of looseness, in evaluating the soundness of our theories, and in knowing how to improve the inner conceptual structure of our theories.

This welcomed direction of development would follow from the careful use of two strategies especially. The main one is the integrative development of substantively new theories of psychotherapeutic practice. Whether this integrative development proceeds by means of theories of psychotherapy that share the same parent theory of human beings or by means of the formulation of a modified theory of human beings, the consequence will be that of a smaller number of distinctive theories of psychotherapy. In addition, a measure of integration will follow from the second strategy which consists of the development and integrative use of a large public pool of concretely specific operating procedures. As therapies make use of this public pool, integration gradually occurs mainly at the ground level of working tools. This avenue would likely yield a limited measure of integration, but some will take place.

It is likely that the therapies that develop will be distinctive mainly because of the differences between their parent theories of human beings. Indeed, I believe that the ceiling on the number of therapies will be the number of distinctive theories of human beings. Accordingly, it seems that, in terms of large families of therapies, we would probably move in the direction of no fewer than three or five families of psychotherapy, with each connected to its own large parental theory of human beings: existential-humanistic, psychoanalytic, social learning, psychobiological, and perhaps one or two others. It will be the number of distinctive theories of human beings that determines the number of integrative psychotherapies. In any case, the consequence is that of a small number of distinctive therapies, with the distinctiveness bestowed by the parental theory of human beings.

In this gradual overall process of integration toward a smaller number of therapies, I foresee two kinds of therapies that will be incorporated into the bigger integrative therapies. One is the many therapies that are perhaps more specialized treatment packages for specialized purposes. I am referring to such specialized programs as assertion training programs, self-control and self-monitoring programs for the reduction of smoking, relaxation training programs, autogenic programs, and the like. While they may retain their packaged usefulness, they will be encompassed within one larger integrative therapy or another, rather than existing free-standing as separate therapies. The second kind of therapy includes those whose identity is predominantly yoked to particular therapeutic stratagems or even operating procedures. A fair number of therapies is included here, therapies with loose theories of psychotherapy, therapies that can attach themselves to various theories of psychotherapy because they really consist mainly of a limited number of things that the therapist does. As integration proceeds, I expect these will also tend to be incorporated into the emerging larger integrative theories of psychotherapy.

A competitive power struggle for superiority.   A second consequence, depending on which strategies predominate, is a competitive power struggle for king of the therapeutic mountain. The contenders will claim that their integrative framework is superior, their vocabulary is to be adopted over others, their version of science and research is predominant, their theory and methods are the best way of integrating and their treatment is most effective as shown by their research carried out within their research paradigm (Mahrer, 1985). It is a competitive struggle in which one or a few will emerge as regnant and the others be relegated to second class. The regnant psychotherapy would likely have one of two characters. It may be a saturine, comprehensive, monolithic philosophical and conceptual giant reigning over the field of psychotherapy. Or it may degenerate into a mushy mélange of loose common denominators across most psychotherapies. In either case, this kind of competitive power struggle is unfortunate for our field, I believe.

I suggest that this consequence will occur when the strategy is that of justifying an integrative super-framework, when the strategy is that of trying to integrate commonalities across various theories of psychotherapies, and when the strategy is that of trying to integrate therapeutic vocabularies by asserting that my vocabulary can incorporate yours.

Mushrooming proliferation of psychotherapies. A third consequence is a mushrooming proliferation in the number of psychotherapies. This would be the likely consequence of the strategy of integrative super-frameworks, the strategy of emphasizing commonalities across psychotherapies, and also the strategy of diagnosing the problem and prescribing the appropriate treatment. If, for example, there are 30 or 50 or 100 different therapies, these strategies would open the gates of integration in so many different ways that the potential numbers of likely future therapies are staggering.

The effects of these strategies would be toward leveling out most psychotherapies, accepting that most therapies are essentially similar to one another, masking genuine differences and highlighting commonalities, and thereby justifying each therapist doing that individual's brand of therapy. The consequence is little development, improvement, or change, and a grand idiosyncrasizing of each therapist's own way of doing therapy. Similarly, as it becomes increasingly apparent that many therapists have many ways of mixing and matching intact approaches in prescribing treatment stratagems, the converging consequence is again mushrooming proliferation.

These are the three major consequences that I believe are likely to occur. In each of the final sections of the preceding chapters I mentioned a few other likely consequences, but these are the three main ones. I regard each of them as very serious for our field. It would have powerful impact on our field if we move toward a small number of sound, distinctive psychotherapies, or if there were a mushrooming proliferation of psychotherapies, or if we were to enter into the kind of competitive power struggle that leaves our field in an undeveloped shambles. I am convinced that one or two of these consequences will indeed occur. Too large a proportion of psychotherapists is explicitly or implicitly engaged in silent integrative strategies to prevent one or more of these consequences from coming about. Fortunately, we can have a hand in determining which of these consequences will occur.

RECOMMENDATIONS

These conclusions may be interesting, but what implications do they bear for what we are to do? If it makes sense to appreciate a distinction between six strategies and meanings of integrating psychotherapies, if some are indeed more useful and workable than others, and if there is some agreement on the likely consequences for the field of psychotherapy, then there are steps that can be taken to move this field of ours forward. I am speaking to the individual practitioner as well as the teacher, supervisor, patient, researcher, and all the others who have a stake in this field of psychotherapy. Accordingly, I have outlined a series of recommendations. I hope they will be seriously considered, modified, and then acted upon.

1. The integrative development of substantive new theories of psychotherapy

1.1. Adoption and use of this strategy. It is recommended that therapists work hard at adopting and using the strategy of integrative development of substantive new theories of psychotherapy. This strategy has promise and should be pursued.

1.2. The formal study of the components and structures of theories of psychotherapy. It is recommended that psychotherapists work toward the development of a field of study that includes the components and structures of theories of psychotherapy. Our theories of psychotherapy are much more than a collection of loose ideas about what human beings are like, and much more than a loose collection of things that therapists do. It is time to take a close look at our theories of psychotherapy as theories, to define and articulate the components of a theory of psychotherapy, to study the formal properties of these theories as we would any other kind of theory. I have proposed a set of components for a theory of psychotherapy, and a set of criteria to assess a theory of psychotherapy as adequate. Offer better alternatives. Get on with the job of developing the formal study of our theories of psychotherapy, of their components and structures.

There are also ways of putting this formal field of study into actual operation. Courses on psychotherapy can include more than the content of the various approaches to psychotherapy. The study of psychotherapy should include the formal inquiry into each theory *as* theory. To what extent do the various approaches include all of the formal components of a theory of psychotherapy? How do these theories fare in a formal comparative assessment of their adequacy and worth as formal theories of psychotherapy? How do theories of psychotherapy compare and contrast on each of the components of a theory of psychotherapy? Articles, chapters, and books on given therapeutic approaches, and especially on new theories and new integrative blendings of theories, should be asked to spell out the specific components of their theory and also to indicate how they fare in regard to the criteria of adequacy and worth of theories of psychotherapy.

1.3. Psychotherapists as personality theorists. It is recommended that psychotherapists be personality theorists, that part of the role of psychotherapist is to be thoroughly knowledgeable in theories of human beings, and that psychotherapists are to contribute to the development of theories of human beings. Theories of human beings are the gateway to the integrative development of new theories of psychotherapy.

2. The integration of concretely specific operating procedures

2.1. Adoption and use of this strategy. It is recommended that each therapy expand its own useable pool of concretely specific operating procedures by borrowing and adopting selected operations from other therapies. This is the second integrative strategy. It is highly recommended.

2.2. Operating procedures versus general therapeutic stratagems. It is recommended that psychotherapists recognize a distinction between (a) the actual working tools of therapy, the nuts and bolts of therapy, the concretely specific working operations (e.g., obtaining demographic data, reflecting the implied feeling, disputing the patient's belief, disclosing something personal about oneself) and, on the other hand, (b) therapeutic programs or general therapeutic stratagems (e.g., dream analysis, assertiveness training, self-exploration, counterconditioning).

2.3. A public pool of operating procedures.   We need a public pool of all the concretely specific operating procedures used in psychotherapy. Worded in a style free of jargon, these operating procedures should be described, perhaps with a few illustrations of each, and maybe even organized into helpful groups. Some would be quite molecular, and some a little bigger, but they would all be part of the actual working nuts and bolts of what therapists do.

2.4. Libraries of psychotherapy tapes.   We need bigger and better libraries of psychotherapy tapes. These should include tapes from every therapeutic approach, tapes of uncommon sessions, sessions that are especially good or especially interesting. We need tapes from therapists who are competent, effective, innovative. We need series of tapes of work with a single patient, sampled over a whole sequence of sessions. These libraries are the raw data we need to study psychotherapy.

3. The integration of therapeutic vocabularies

3.1. Adoption and use of the little meaning.   It is recommended that therapists and clinical researchers adopt and use the strategy of identifying and integrating terms sharing the same psychotherapeutic referent event. While the degree of integration here is probably rather limited, the enterprise is worthwhile and should be pursued.

3.2. Abandon use of the big meaning.   It is recommended that therapists and clinical researchers abandon efforts at trying to develop a single common therapeutic vocabulary.

4. The integrative super-framework

4.1. Abandon the integrative super-framework strategy. It is recommended that therapists abandon the strategy of trying to elevate some current therapy into the status of super-framework, and of trying to construct new super-frameworks. Super-frameworks are infeasible and unworkable, and the whole enterprise should be abandoned.

5. Integrating commonalities across approaches

5.1. Abandon the strategy of integrating commonalities across approaches. It is recommended that therapists abandon the strategy of trying to integrate commonalities across psychotherapies. Whatever genuine commonalities may be present will contribute to integration in the course of the three strategies recommended above.

6. Diagnose-the-problem and prescribe-the-treatment

6.1. Abandon the strategy of diagnosing-the-problem and pre-scribing-the-treatment. It is recommended that therapists abandon the strategy of diagnosing a problem and then prescribing an appropriate treatment from a pool of therapeutic approaches. As a general strategy, it is infeasible and unworkable.

6.2. Putting "the problem" in its appropriate place. It is recommended that efforts at defining a problem that therapy is to "treat" be abandoned as a universally appropriate enterprise, and that these efforts be connected only to those therapeutic approaches for which this meaning of therapy *is* appropriate. Even within those approaches that seek to identify a problem to be treated, the specific content of the nature of the problem will vary with the given theory of psychotherapy. Accordingly, (a) research studying therapeutic change and outcome should identify the particular theory or theories of psychotherapy for which the designated "problem" is appropriate, and (b) clinical discussion of any designated "problem" should likewise identify the particular theory or theories of psychotherapy for whom that designated problem is appropriate, and for whom therapy is limited to the "treatment" of that "problem." The heart of this recommendation is that some therapies include much more than treatment of some designated problem.

6.3. Putting the "standard intake evaluation" in its appropriate place.   It is recommended that the "standard intake evaluation" or diagnostic assessment be used only in those therapies for which it is conceptually and clinically appropriate. If the sixth strategy is abandoned, some of the basis for this unfortunately widespread procedure will evaporate, and the use of standard intake evaluations and diagnostic assessments will be limited to those therapies which call for such a procedure.

7. Education and training in psychotherapy

7.1. Students should know about the integration of psychotherapies.   It is recommended that the general issues and knowledge having to do with the integration of psychotherapies be a part of the education and training of psychotherapists. Regardless of the degree and of the discipline, some acquaintance with the integration of psychotherapies should be incorporated into the education and training programs.

7.2. No theory is basic or foundational.   It is recommended that psychotherapy training programs abandon teaching of a given theory or approach to psychotherapy as basic or foundational. There is no hierarchy of psychotherapies such that a given one is to be taught first or regarded as requisite to the later teaching of others. There is no integrative super-theory. There is no basic or foundational theory or approach to psychotherapy. Whatever classification or organizational system is used for the various theories and approaches to psychotherapy, no one theory or approach is to be regarded as basic or foundational to the others. For example, if theories and approaches are organized into humanistic-experiential, psychoanalytic-psychodynamic, behavioral, and even eclectic-integrative, no one of these is to be required or taught first as basic or foundational to the others. There are no basic or foundational kinds of useful material to be elicited, no basic or foundational ways of listening/observing what patients say and do, no basic or foundational way of describing patients and defining the target of change, no basic or foundational therapeutic goals and directions of change, no basic or foundational principles of therapeutic change, no basic or foundational general therapeutic stratagems. Trying to impose some theory or approach as basic or foundational is merely another manifestation of the competition among therapies for super status. It should be abandoned.

7.3. The learning of multiple approaches to theoretical issues. It is recommended that psychotherapy students learn multiple approaches to those issues that are ordinarily protected as single truths. This goes well beyond the standard courses in the major theories, approaches, and schools of psychotherapy. Instead, this recommendation points toward the students learning that the very identification of a "problem" is a complex process varying enormously from theory to theory. It points toward the students learning that their very way of listening to and observing the patient, what the patient says and does, is a complicated process of selecting and using one mode of listening/observing from a number of modes. It means that students are to learn that virtually everything they may accept as basic, universal, foundational, invariant, obvious, and real is so only *within* some given theoretical approach.

7.4. An understandable emphasis on those theories of psychotherapy whose parent theories of human beings are germane to the particular psychotherapy-related discipline. It is recommended that each psychotherapy-related discipline emphasize those theories of psychotherapy whose parental theories of human beings are germane to that discipline. I am presuming that psychotherapy training occurs in various disciplines such a psychology, psychiatry, social work, education, pastoral counseling, nursing, human relations, and other disciplines. My recommendation is that each discipline say in effect that we emphasize a particular theory or theories of human beings, and that we therefore emphasize theories of psychotherapy that are consistent with that or these theories of human beings—although there are other theories of human beings and other theories of psychotherapy. This is an understandable limitation. For example, the theories of human beings emphasized by the discipline of psychiatry may not include existential-humanistic theories of human beings, and I can understand that training programs in psychiatry do not highlight experiential psycotherapy.

7.5. Postdoctoral training centers in psychotherapy.   It is recommended that training in advanced knowledge and competence in a given psychotherapeutic approach be the province of postdoctoral training centers in psychotherapy. Leaving aside the thorny issue of masters versus doctoral level training, the whole matter of integration of psychotherapies leaves me even more inclined to favor postdoctoral training centers as the appropriate site for advanced knowledge and competence in a given psychotherapeutic approach. I am convinced that masters and doctoral training programs in any or all of the psychotherapy-related professions should make sure that their students are quite familiar with all the issues having to do with the integration of psychotherapies. This is merely another reason why the gaining of genuinely sound and solid advanced knowledge and competence in some explicit therapeutic approach ought to be the job of fine postdoctoral (or at least postgraduate) training centers in, e.g., experiential psychotherapy, psychoanalytic therapy, behavior therapy, Jungian therapy, and the like.

8. Psychotherapy research

8.1. Conditions-operations-consequences.   It is recommended that researchers accept and use the conditions-operations-consequences schema for studying psychotherapy. That is, researchers study the relationships between working therapeutic conditions (e.g., when the patient is being this way or that way), therapeutic operations (e.g., carrying out this concretely specific operating procedure), and therapeutic consequences (e.g., this in-session welcomed and desirable event). The more we adopt and use the first integrative strategy and the more we examine theories of psychotherapy in terms of their components, the closer we come to studying psychotherapy in terms of conditions-operations-consequences.

8.2. Psychotherapy tapes. It is recommended that researchers welcome the direct study of psychotherapy tapes. The second strategy (the integration of concretely specific operating procedures) especially calls for the establishment of libraries of psychotherapy tapes, and also for study of psychotherapy at the level of actual working operations.

8.3. The thoughtful study of psychotherapy by psychotherapists. It is recommended that the meaning of research be extended to include the thoughtful, penetrating, analytic, scholarly inquiry of psychotherapy by psychotherapists. As we confront issues raised by integrationists, it seems to me that we need even more the assistance of fine thinking clinicians who can add their own distinctive kind of research inquiry. Careful, rigorous research into psychotherapy can go beyond sophisticated designs, statistics, and technology.

8.4. Discovery-oriented as well as hypothesis-testing research. It is recommended that researchers achieve a balance between discovery-oriented and hypothesis-testing research. In the field of psychotherapy, most of our research consists of the testing of hypotheses. The integrative movement is inviting us to adopt a complementary research strategy that is oriented toward the discovery of knowledge and the framing of data-generated new hypotheses. I urge psychotherapy researchers to adopt and use discovery-oriented research strategies that are as toughly rigorous as those used in hypothesis-testing research, but which carry the added advantage of discovering more about psychotherapy.

Integration among psychotherapies is occurring. We are in a position to guide this movement in ways that are helpful for our field. I hope that you seriously consider these conclusions and recommendations, and that you follow the recommendations that make sense to you. In any case, I welcome your correspondence. Please do write to me.

REFERENCES

Alexander, F. (1963). The dynamics of psychotherapy in the light of learning theory. *American Journal of Psychiatry, 5,* 440–448.

Alexander, F., & French, T.M. (1964). *Psychoanalytic theory.* New York: Ronald.

Arkowitz, H., & Messer, S.B. (Eds.) (1984). *Psychoanalytic therapy and behavior therapy: Is integration possible?* New York and London: Plenum.

Arnkoff, D.B. (1980). Psychotherapy from the perspective of cognitive theory. In M.J. Mahoney (Ed.) *Psychotherapy process.* New York: Plenum.

Bandura, A. (1977). Self-efficacy: Toward a unifying theory of behavioral change. *Psychological Review, 84,* 191–215.

Bergin, A.E., & Lambert, M.J. (1978). The evaluation of therapeutic outcomes. In A.E. Bergin & S.L. Garfield (Eds.) *Handbook of psychotherapy and behavior change: An empirical analysis,* 2nd ed. New York: John Wiley.

Bernstein, S. (1984). A case history demonstrating the complementary use of psychodynamic and behavioral techniques in therapy. *Psychotherapy, 21,* 402–407.

Beutler, L.E. (1983). *Eclectic psychotherapy: A systematic approach.* New York: Pergamon.

Beutler, L.E. (1986). Systematic eclectic psychotherapy. In J.C. Norcross (Ed.) *Handbook of eclectic psychotherapy.* New York: Brunner/Mazel.

Birk, L. (1970). Behavior therapy: Integration with dynamic psychiatry. *Behavior Therapy, 1,* 522–526.

Birk, L., & Brinkley-Birk, A. (1974). Psychoanalysis and behavior therapy. *The American Journal of Psychiatry, 131,* 449–509.

Brady, J.P. (1968). Psychotherapy by combined behavioral and dynamic approach. *Comprehensive Psychiatry, 9,* 536–543.

Brown, B.M. (1967). Cognitive aspects of Wolpe's behavior therapy. *American Journal of Psychiatry, 124,* 854–859.

Cohen, I.H. & Pope, B. (1980). Concurrent use of insight and desensitization therapy. *Psychiatry, 43,* 146–154.

Dewald, P.A. (1971). *Psychotherapy: A dynamic approach,* 2nd ed. New York: Basic Books.

Diamond, R.E., Havens, R.A., & Jones, A.C. (1978). A conceptual framework for the practice of prescriptive eclecticism in psychotherapy. *American Psychologist, 33,* 239–248.

Dollard, J. & Miller, J.E. (1950). *Personality and psychotherapy.* New York: McGraw-Hill.

Driscoll, R. (1984). *Pragmatic psychotherapy.* New York: Van Nostrand Reinhold.

Driscoll, R. (1987). Ordinary language as common thought. *Journal of Integrative and Eclectic Psychotherapy.*

Dryden, W. (1986). Eclectic psychotherapies: A critique of leading approaches. In J.C. Norcross (Ed.) *Handbook of eclectic psychotherapy.* New York: Brunner/Mazel.

Elliott, R., Stiles, W.B., Shiffman, S., Barker, C.B., Burstein, B., & Goodman, G. (1982). The empirical analysis of helping communication: Conceptual framework and recent research. In T.A. Wills (Ed.) *Basic processes in helping relationships.* New York: Academic Press.

Ellis, A. (1976). Rational-Emotive Therapies. In V. Binder, A. Binder, & B. Rimland (Eds.) *Modern Therapies.* Englewood Cliffs, New Jersey: Prentice-Hall.

Ellis, A. (1979). *Reason and emotion in psychotherapy.* Secaucus, New Jersey: Citadel.

Feather, B.W., & Rhoads, J.M. (1972). Psychodynamic behavior therapy. *Archives of General Psychiatry, 26,* 496–511.

Feigl, H. (1953). The mind-body problem in the development of logical empiricism. In H. Feigl & M. Brodbeck (Eds.) *Readings in the philosophy of science.* New York: Appleton-Century-Crofts.

Fiske, D.W. (1971). *Measuring the concepts of personality.* Chicago: Aldine.

Forsyth, D.R. & Strong, S.R. (1986). The scientific study of counseling and psychotherapy: A unificationist view. *American Psychologist, 41,* 113–119.

Frank, J.D. (1973). *Persuasion and healing: A comparative study of psychotherapy.* Baltimore: Johns Hopkins University Press.

Frank, J.D. (1982). Therapeutic components shared by all psychotherapies. In J.H. Harvey, & M.M. Parks (Eds.) *Psychotherapy research and behavior change.* Washington, D.C.: American Psychological Association.

Frankel, A.J. (1984). *Four therapies integrated.* Englewood Cliffs, New Jersey: Prentice-Hall.

Franks, C.M. (1984). On conceptual and technical integrity in psychoanalysis and behavior therapy: Two fundamentally incompatible systems. In H. Arkowitz & S.B. Messer (Eds.) *Psychoanalytic therapy and behavior therapy: Is integration possible?* New York and London: Plenum.

Franks, C.M., & Wilson, G.T. (1979). Behavior change: An overview. In C.M. Franks & G.T. Wilson (Eds.) *Annual review of behavior therapy.* New York: Brunner/Mazel.

French, T.M. (1933). Interrelations between psychoanalysis and the experimental work of Pavlov. *American Journal of Psychiatry, 89,* 1165–1203.

Fuhriman, A., Paul, S.C., & Burlingame, G.M. (1986). Eclectic time-limited therapy. In J.C. Norcross (Ed.) *Handbook of eclectic psychotherapy.* New York: Brunner/Mazel.

Garfield, S.L. (1980). *Psychotherapy: An eclectic approach.* New York: Wiley.

Garfield, S.L. (1986). An eclectic psychotherapy. In J.C. Norcross (Ed.) *Handbook of eclectic psychotherapy.* New York: Brunner/Mazel.

Garfield, S.L., & Kurz, R. A. (1976). Clinical psychologists in the 1970's, *American Psychologist, 31,* 1–9.

Garfield, S.L., & Kurz, R.A. (1977). A study of eclectic views. *Journal of Consulting and Clinical Psychology, 45,* 78–83.

Gelso, C.J., & Carter, J.A. (1985). The relationship in counseling and psychotherapy: Components, consequences, and theoretical antecedents. *The Counseling Psychologist, 13,* 155–243.

Gendlin, E.T. (1986). What comes after traditional psychotherapy research? *American Psychologist, 41,* 131–136.

Gervaize, P.A., Mahrer, A.R., & Markow, R. Therapeutic laughter: What therapists do to promote strong laughter in patients. *Psychotherapy in Private Practice, 3,* 65–74.

Gill, M.M. (1984). Psychoanalytic, psychodynamic, cognitive behavior, and behavior therapies compared. In H. Arkowitz & S.B. Messer (Ed.) *Psychoanalytic therapy and behavior change: Is integration possible?* New York and London: Plenum.

Goldfried, M.R. (1980). Toward the delineation of therapeutic change principles. *American Psychologist, 35,* 991–999.

Goldfried, M.R. (Ed.) (1982b). *Converging themes in psychotherapy.* New York: Springer.

Goldfried, M.R. (1987). A common language for the psychotherapies: Commentary. *Journal of Integrative and Eclectic Psychotherapy.*

Goldfried, M.R., & Newman, C. (1986). Psychotherapy integration: An historical perspective. In J.C. Norcross (Ed.) *Handbook of eclectic psychotherapy.* New York: Brunner/Mazel.

Goldfried, M.R., & Padawer, W. (1982). Current status and future directions in psychotherapy. In M.R. Goldfried (Ed.) *Converging themes in psychotherapy.* New York: Springer.

Goldfried, M.R., & Safran, J.D. (1986). Future directions in psychotherapy integration. In J.C. Norcross (Ed.) *Handbook of eclectic psychotherapy.* New York: Brunner/Mazel.

Goldstein, A.P., & Stein, N. (1976). *Prescriptive psychotherapies.* New York: Pergamon.

Gomes-Schwartz, B. (1978). Effective ingredients in psychotherapy: Prediction of outcome from process variables. *Journal of Consulting and Clinical Psychology, 46,* 1023–1035.

Goodman, G., & Dooley, D. (1976). A framework for help-intended communication. *Psychotherapy: Theory, Research and Practice, 13,* 106–117.

Greenson, R.R. (1965). The working alliance and transference neurosis. *Psychoanalytic Quarterly, 34,* 158–181.

Greenson, R.R. (1967). *The technique and practice of psychoanalysis* (Vol. 1). New York: International Universities Press.

Grinker, R.R. (1976). Discussion of Strupp's "Some critical comments on the future of psychoanalytic therapy". *Bulletin of Menninger Clinic, 40,* 247–254.

Halgin, R.P. (1985). Teaching integration of psychotherapy models to beginning therapists. *Psychotherapy, 22,* 555–563.

Hart, J. (1983). *Modern eclectic therapy.* New York: Plenum

Held, B.S. (1984). Toward a strategic eclecticism: A proposal. *Psychotherapy: 21,* 232–241.

Hill, C.E. (1983). Counseling process research: Philosophical and methodological dilemmas. *Counseling Psychologist, 10,* 7–19.

Jacoby, R. (1975). *Social amnesia.* Boston: Beacon Press.

Jayaratne, S. (1982). Characteristics and theoretical orientations of clinical social workers: A national survey. *Journal of Social Service Research, 4,* 17–30.

Kantor, J.R. (1953). *The logic of modern science.* Bloomingdale, Illinois: Principia Press.

Kazdin, A.E. (1984). Integration of psychodynamic and behavioral psychotherapies: Conceptual versus empirical syntheses, In H. Arkowitz & S.B. Messer (Eds.) *Psychoanalytic therapy and behavior therapy: Is integration possible?* New York and London: Plenum.

Koch, S. (1964). Psychology and emerging conceptions of knowledge as unitary. In T.W. Wann (Ed.) *Behaviorism and phenomenology: Contrasting bases for modern psychology.* Chicago: University of Chicago Press.

Koch, S. (1981). The nature and limits of psychological knowledge: Lessons of a century qua "science." *American Psychologist, 36,* 257–269.

Krasner, L. (1968). Discussion. In R. Porter (Ed.) *Ciba symposium: The role of learning in psychotherapy.* London: Churchill.

Krasner, L. (1978). The future and the past in the behaviorism-humanism dialogue. *American Psychologist, 33,* 799–804.

Lazarus, A.A. (1967). In support of technical eclecticism. *Psychological Reports, 21,* 415–416.

Lazarus, A.A. (1976). *Multi-modal behavior therapy.* New York: Springer.

Lazarus, A.A. (1981). *The practice of multimodal therapy.* New York: McGraw-Hill.

Lazarus, A.A. (Ed.) (1985). *Casebook of multimodal therapy.* New York: Guilford.

Leitner, L.M. (1982). Literalism, perspectivism, chaotic fragmentation, and psychotherapy techniques. *British Journal of Medical Psychology, 55,* 307–317.

Levis, D.J. (1970). Integration of behavior therapy and dynamic psychiatric techniques: A marriage with a high probability of ending in divorce. *Behavior Therapy, 1,* 531–537.

London, P. (1964). *The modes and morals of psychotherapy.* New York: Holt, Rinehart, and Winston.

Luborsky, L. (1976). Helping alliance in psychotherapy. In J. L. Claghorn (Ed.) *Successful psychotherapy.* New York: Brunner/Mazel.

Luborsky, L. (1985). Psychotherapy integration is on its way. *Journal of Counseling Psychotherapy, 13,* 245–249l.

Mahrer, A.R. (1962). A preface to the mind-body problem. *Psychological Record, 12,* 53–60.

Mahrer, A.R. (1967). The goals and families of psychotherapy: Discussion. In A.R. Mahrer (Ed.) *The goals of psychotherapy.* New York: Appleton-Century-Crofts.

Mahrer, A.R. (1976). Some known effects of psychotherapy and a reinterpretation. In A.G. Banet, Jr. (Ed.) *Creative psychotherapy: A source book.* La Jolla, California: University Associates.

Mahrer, A.R. (1978a). *Experiencing: A humanistic theory of psychology and psychiatry.* New York: Brunner/Mazel.

Mahrer, A.R. (1978b). Sequence and consequence in the experiential psychotherapies. In C. Cooper & C. Alderfer (Eds.) *Advances in experiential social processes.* New York: Wiley.

Mahrer, A.R. (1978c). The therapist-patient relationship: Conceptual analysis and a proposal for a paradigm-shift. *Psychotherapy: Theory, Research and Practice, 15,* 201–215.

Mahrer, A.R. (1979). An invitation to theoreticians and researchers from an applied experiential practitioner. *Psychotherapy: Theory, Research and Practice, 16,* 409–418.

Mahrer, A.R. (1980). Research on theoretical concepts of psychotherapy. In W. DeMoor & H.R. Wijngaarden (Eds.) *Psychotherapy: Research and training.* Amsterdam: Elsevier/North Holland Biomedical Press.

Mahrer, A.R. (1983a). *Experiential psychotherapy: Basic practices.* New York: Brunner/Mazel.

Mahrer, A.R. (1983b). An existential-experiential view and operational perspective on passive-aggressiveness. In R.D. Parsons and R.J. Wicks (Eds.) *Passive aggressiveness: Theory and practice.* New York: Brunner/Mazel.

Mahrer, A.R. (1983c). Taxonomy of procedures and operations in psychotherapy. Unpublished manuscript, School of Psychology, University of Ottawa, Ottawa, Canada K1N 6N5.

Mahrer, A.R. (1984). The care and feeding of abrasiveness. *The Psychotherapy Patient, 1,* 69–78.

Mahrer, A.R. (1985). *Psychotherapeutic change: An alternative approach to meaning and measurement.* New York: Norton.

Mahrer, A.R. (1986a). *Therapeutic experiencing: The process of change.* New York: Norton.

Mahrer, A.R. (1986b). A challenge to communication therapy: The therapist does not communicate with the patient. *Journal of Communication Therapy, 3,* 97–114.

Mahrer, A.R. (1987). These are the components of any theory of psychotherapy. *Journal of Integrative and Eclectic Psychotherapy, 6,* 28–31.

Mahrer, A.R. (in press). If there really were a specialty of psychotherapy: Standards for postdoctoral training in psychotherapy. *The Humanistic Psychologist.*

Mahrer, A.R. (in press). The case for fundamentally different existential-humanistic psychologies. *Journal of Humanistic Psychology.*

Mahrer, A.R., Brown, S.D., Gervaize, P.A., & Fellers, G. (1983). Reflection, self-exploration, and client-therapist communication: Some unexpected in-therapy consequences. *Journal of Communication Therapy, 2,* 1–13.

Mahrer, A.R., & Boulet, D.B. (1986). An experiential session with Edward and his "obsessional" thoughts and fears. *The Psychotherapy Patient, 3,* 143–158.

Mahrer, A.R., Clark, E.L., Comeau, L., & Brunette, A. (in press). Therapist-Statements as prescriptions-for-change. *Journal of Communication Therapy.*

Mahrer, A.R., & Gervaize, P.A. (1983). Impossible roles therapist must play. *Canadian Psychology, 24,* 81–87.

Mahrer, A.R., & Gervaize, P.A. (1986). The steps and methods in experiential psychotherapy sessions. In P.A. Keller & L.G. Ritt (Eds.). *Innovations in clinical practice: A source book,* vol. 5. Sarasota, Florida: Professional Resource Exchange.

Mahrer, A.R., & Nadler, W.P. (1986). Good moments in psychotherapy: A preliminary review, a list, and some promising research avenues. *Journal of Consulting and Clinical Psychology, 54,* 10–16.

Mahrer, A.R., Nadler, W.P., Dessaulles, A., & Gervaize, P.A. (1987). Good and very good moments in psychotherapy. Content, distribution, and facilitation. *Psychotherapy, 24,* 7–14.

Mahrer, A.R., Nadler, W.P. Gervaize, P.A., & Markow, R. (1986). Discovering how one therapist obtains some very good moments in psychotherapy. *Voices: The Art and Science of Psychotherapy, 22,* 72–83.

Mahrer, A.R., Nifakis, D.J., Abhukara, L., & Sterner, I. (1984). Microstrategies in psychotherapy: The patterning of sequential statements. *Psychotherapy, 21,* 465–472.

Mahrer, A.R., Paterson, W.E., Thériault, A.T., Roessler, C., & Quenneville, A. (1986). How and why to use a large number of clinically sophisticated judges in psychotherapy research. *Voices: The Art and Science of Psychotherapy.*

Mahrer, A.R., & Pearson, L. (1973). The working processes of psychotherapy. In A.R. Mahrer & L. Pearson (Eds.) *Creative developments in psychotherapy.* New York: Jason Aronson.

Mahrer, A.R., Sterner, I., Lawson, K.C., & Dessaulles, A. (1986). Microstrategies: Distinctively patterned sequences of therapist statements. *Psychotherapy, 23,* 50–56.

Marmor, J. (1971). Dynamic psychotherapy and behavior therapy: Are they irreconcilable? *Archives of General Psychiatry, 24,* 22–28.

Marmor, J. (1976). Common operational factors in diverse approaches to behavior change. In A. Burton (Ed.) *What makes behavior change possible?* New York: Brunner/Mazel.

Marmor, J., & Woods, S.M. (1980). *The interface between psychodynamic and behavioral therapies.* New York: Plenum.

Merluzzi, T.V., Rudy, T.E., & Glass, C.R. (1981). The information processing paradigm: Implications for clinical science. In T.V. Merluzzi, C.R. Glass, & M. Genest (Eds.) *Cognitive assessment.* New York: Guilford Press.

Messer, S.B. (1986). Eclecticism in psychotherapy: Underlying assumptions, problems, and trade-offs. In J.C. Norcross (Ed.) *Handbook of eclectic psychotherapy.* New York: Brunner/Mazel.

Messer, S.B. (1987). Can the tower of Babel be completed: A critique of the common language proposal. *Journal of Integrative and Eclectic Psychotherapy, 6,* 227–234.

Messer, S.B., & Winokur, M. (1980). Some limits to the integration of psychoanalytic and behavior therapy. *American Psychologist, 35,* 818–827.

Messer, S.B., & Winokur, M. (1984). Ways of knowing and visions of reality in psychoanalytic therapy and behavior therapy. In H. Arkowitz & S.B. Messer (Eds.) *Psychoanalytic therapy and behavior therapy: Is integration possible?* New York and London: Plenum Press.

Mintz, J., Auerbach, A.H., Luborsky, L., & Johnson, M. (1973). Patients', therapists', and observers' views of psychotherapy: A "Rashomon" experience or a reasonable consensus? *British Journal of Medical Psychology, 46,* 83–89.

Murgatroyd, S., & Apter, M.J. (1986). A structural-phenomenological approach to eclectic psychotherapy. In J.C. Norcross (Ed.) *Handbook of eclectic psychotherapy.* New York: Brunner/Mazel.

Nash, J., Norcross, J.C., & Prochaska, J.O. (1984). Satisfactions and stresses of independent practice. *Psychotherapy in Private Practice, 2,* 39–48.

Norcross, J.C. (Ed.) (1986a). *Handbook of eclectic psychotherapy.* New York: Brunner/Mazel.

Norcross, J.C. (1986b). Beginnings. *Journal of Integrative and Eclectic Psychotherapy, 5,* 3–4.

Norcross, J.C. (1986c). Eclectic psychotherapy: An introduction and overview. In J.C. Norcross (Ed.) *Handbook of eclectic psychotherapy,* New York: Brunner/Mazel.

Norcross, J.C. (1987). Toward a common language for psychotherapy: An introduction. *Journal of Integrative and Electic Psychotherapy, 6,* 180–184.

Norcross, J.C., Beutler, L.E., Clarkin, J.F., DiClemente, C.C., Halgin, R.P., Frances, A., Prochaska, J.O., Robertson, M., & Suedfield, P. (1986). Training integrative/eclectic psychotherapists. *Journal of Integrative and Eclectic Psychotherapy, 5,* 71–95.

Norcross, J.C., & Prochaska, J.O. (1982). A national survey of clinical psychologists: Affiliations and orientations. *The Clinical Psychologist, 35,* 4–6.

Orlinsky, D.E., & Howard, K.I. (1977). The therapist's experience of psychotherapy. In A.S. Gurman & A.M. Razin (Eds.) *Effective psychotherapy: A handbook of research.* New York: Pergamon.

Orlinsky, D.E., & Howard, K.I. (1978). The relation of process to outcome in psychotherapy. In S.L. Garfield & A.E. Bergin (Eds.) *Handbook of psychotherapy and behavior change: An empirical analysis* (2nd ed.). New York: Wiley.

Orlinsky, D.E., & Howard, K.I. (1987). A generic model of psychotherapy. *Journal of Integrative and Eclectic Psychotherapy, 6,* 6–27.

Palmer, J.O. (1980). *A primer of eclectic psychotherapy.* Monterey, California: Brooks/Cole.

Parloff, M.B. (1979). Can psychotherapy research guide the policymaker? *American Psychologist, 34,* 296–306.

Paul, G.L. (1967). Strategy of outcome research in psychotherapy. *Journal of Consulting Psychology, 31,* 109–118.

Prochaska, J.O. (1979). *Systems of psychotherapy: A transtheoretical analysis.* Homewood, Illinois: Dorsey.

Prochaska, J.O., & DiClemente, C.C. (1982). Transtheoretical therapy: Toward a more integrative model of change. *Psychotherapy: Theory, Research and Practice, 19,* 276–288.

Prochaska, J.O., & DiClemente, C.C. (1984). *The transtheoretical approach: Crossing the traditional boundaries of psychotherapy.* Homewood, Illinois: Dow Jones-Irvin.

Prochaska, J.O., & Norcross, J.C. (1982). The future of psychotherapy: A Delphi Poll. *Professional Psychology, 13,* 620–627.

Prochaska, J.O., & Norcross, J.C. (1983). Contemporary psychotherapists: A national survey of characteristics, practices, orientations, and attitudes. *Psychotherapy: Theory, Research and Practice, 20,* 161–173.

Rachman, S. (1970). Behavior therapy and psychodynamics. *Behavior Therapy, 1,* 527–530.

Reisman, J.M. (1975). Trends for training in treatment. *Professional Psychology, 6,* 187–192.

Rhoads, J.M., & Feather, B.W. (1972). Transference and resistance observed in behavior therapy. *British Journal of Medical Psychology, 45,* 99–103.

Rhoads, J.M., & Feather, B.F. (1974). The application of psychodynamics to behavior therapy. *American Journal of Psychiatry, 131,* 17–20.

Rosenzweig, S. (1936). Some implicit common factors in diverse methods in psychotherapy. *American Journal of Orthopsychiatry, 6,* 412–415. Also reprinted in M.R. Goldfried (Ed.) *Converging themes in psychotherapy* (1982). New York: Springer.

Royce, J.R. (1982). Philosophy issues, division 24, and the future. *American Psychologist, 37,* 258–266.

Russell, R.L. & Stiles, W.B. (1979). Categories for classifying language in psychotherapy. *Psychological Bulletin, 86,* 404–419.

Ryle, A.A. (1978). A common language for the psychotherapies? *British Journal of Psychiatry, 132,* 585–594.

Ryle, A.A. (1982). *Psychotherapy: A cognitive integration of theory and practice.* London: Academic Press.

Ryle, A.A. (1984). How can we compare different psychotherapies? Why are they all effective? *British Journal of Medical Psychology, 57,* 261–264.

Ryle, A.A. (1987). Cognitive psychology as a common language for psychotherapy. *Journal of Integrative and Eclectic Psychotherapy, 6,* 191–212.

Sarason, J.G. (1979). Three lacunae of cognitive therapy. *Cognitive Therapy and Research, 3,* 223–235.

Schacht, T.E. (1984). The varieties of integrative experience. In Arkowitz & S.B. Messer (Eds.) *Psychoanalytic therapy and behavior therapy: Is integration possible?* New York and London: Plenum Press.

Shemberg, K.M. & Leventhal, D.B. (1978). A survey of activities of academic clinicians. *Professional Psychology, 9,* 580–586.

Silverman, L.H. (1974). Some psychoanalytic considerations of non-psychoanalytic therapies: On the possibility of integrating treatment approaches and related issues. *Psychotherapy: Theory, Research and Practice, 11,* 298–305.

Sloane, R.B., Staples, F.R., Cristol, A.H., Yorkston, N.J., & Whipple, K. (1975). *Short-term analytically oriented psychotherapy vs. behavior therapy.* Cambridge: Harvard University Press.

Smith, D.S. (1982). Trends in counseling and psychotherapy. *American Psychologist, 37,* 802–809.

Smith, D.S., & Kraft, W.A. (1983). DSM-III: Do psychologists really want an alternative? *American Psychologist, 38,* 777–785.

Smith, V.L., & Glass, G.V. (1977). Meta-analysis of psychotherapy outcome studies. *American Psychologist, 32,*752–760.

Smith, M.L., Glass, G.V. & Miller, T.I. (1980). *The benefits of therapy.* Baltimore: Johns Hopkins University Press.

Stiles, W.B., Shapiro, D.A., & Elliott, R. (1986). "Are all psychotherapies equivalent?" *American Psychologist, 41,* 165–180.

Strupp, H.H. (1979). A psychodynamicist looks at modern behavior therapy. *Psychotherapy: Theory, Research and Practice, 16,* 124–131.

Strupp, H.H. (1986). Psychotherapy: Research, practice, and public policy (how to avoid dead ends). *American Psychologist, 41,* 120–130.

Thomas, R.M. (1985). The humanistic perspectives of Maslow, Buhler, and Mahrer. In R.M. Thomas, *Comparing theories of child development*, 2nd ed. Belmont, California: Wadsworth.

Thorne, F.C. (1967). *Integrative psychology*. Brandon, Vermont: Clinical Psychology Publishing Company.

Thorne, F.C. (1980). Eclectic psychotherapy. In R. Herink (Ed.) *The psychotherapy handbook*. New York: New American Library.

Trower, P. & Turkland, D. (1982). Social phobia. In S.M. Turner (Ed.) *Behavioral treatment of anxiety disorders*. New York: Plenum Press.

Trower, P. & Turland, D. (1982). Social phobia. In S.M. Turner (Ed.) *Behavioral treatment of anxiety disorders*. New York: Plenum Press.

Turk, D.C. & Speers, M.A. (1983). Cognitive schemata and cognitive processes in cognitive behavior modification: Going beyond the information given. In P.C. Kendall (Ed.) *Advances in cognitive-behavioral research and therapy*, 2nd ed. volume 2. New York: Academic Press.

Urban, H.B. & Ford, D.H. (1971). Some historical and conceptual perspectives on psychotherapy and behavior change. In A.E. Bergin & S.L. Garfield (Eds.) *Handbook of psychotherapy and behavior change: An empirical analysis*. New York: Wiley.

Wachtel, P.L. (1977). *Psychoanalysis and behavior therapy*. New York: Basic Books.

Wachtel, P.L. (1978). Internal and external determinants of behavior in psychodynamic theories. In L.A. Pervin & M. Lewis (Eds.) *Perspectives in interactional psychology*. New York: Plenum Press.

Wachtel, P.L. (1981). Transference, schema, and assimilation: The relevance of Piaget to the psychoanalytic theory of transference. In J. Miller (Ed.) *The annual of psychoanalysis,* volume 8. New York: International Universities Press.

Wachtel, P.L. (1982a). What can dynamic therapies contribute to behavior therapy? *Behavior Therapy, 13,* 594–609.

Wachtel, P.L. (1982b). Resistance and the process of therapeutic change. In P.L. Wachtel (Ed.) *Resistance: Psychodynamic and behavioral approaches*. New York: Plenum Press.

Wachtel, P.L. (1984). On theory, practice, and the nature of integration. In H. Arkowitz & S.B. Messer (Eds.) *Psychoanalytic therapy and behavior therapy: Is integration possible?* New York and London: Plenum Press.

Weinberg, N.H. & Zaslow, M. (1963). Resistance to systematic desensitization of phobias. *Journal of Clinical Psychology, 19*, 179–181.

Weitzman, B. (1967). *Behavior therapy and psychotherapy.* Psychological Review, 74, 300–317.

Wilkins, W. (1971). Desensitization: Social and cognitive factors underlying the effectiveness of Wolpe's procedure. *Psychological Bulletin, 76*, 311–317.

Wilson, G.T. & Evans, I.M. (1976). Adult behavior therapy and the therapist-client relationship. In C.M. Franks & G.T. Wilson (Eds.) *Annual review of behavior therapy,* volume 4. New York: Brunner/Mazel.

Wilson, G.T. & Evans, I.M. (1977). The therapist-client relationship in behavior therapy. In A.S. Gurman & A.M. Razin (Eds.) *The therapist's contribution to effective psychotherapy: An empirical approach.* New York: Pergamon.

INDEX